# T·H·E
# *Authoritative*
# CALVIN
## AND
# HOBBES

## Other Books by Bill Watterson

*Calvin and Hobbes*
*Something Under the Bed Is Drooling*
*Yukon Ho!*
*Weirdos From Another Planet!*

## Treasury Collections

*The Essential Calvin and Hobbes*
*The Calvin and Hobbes Lazy Sunday Book*

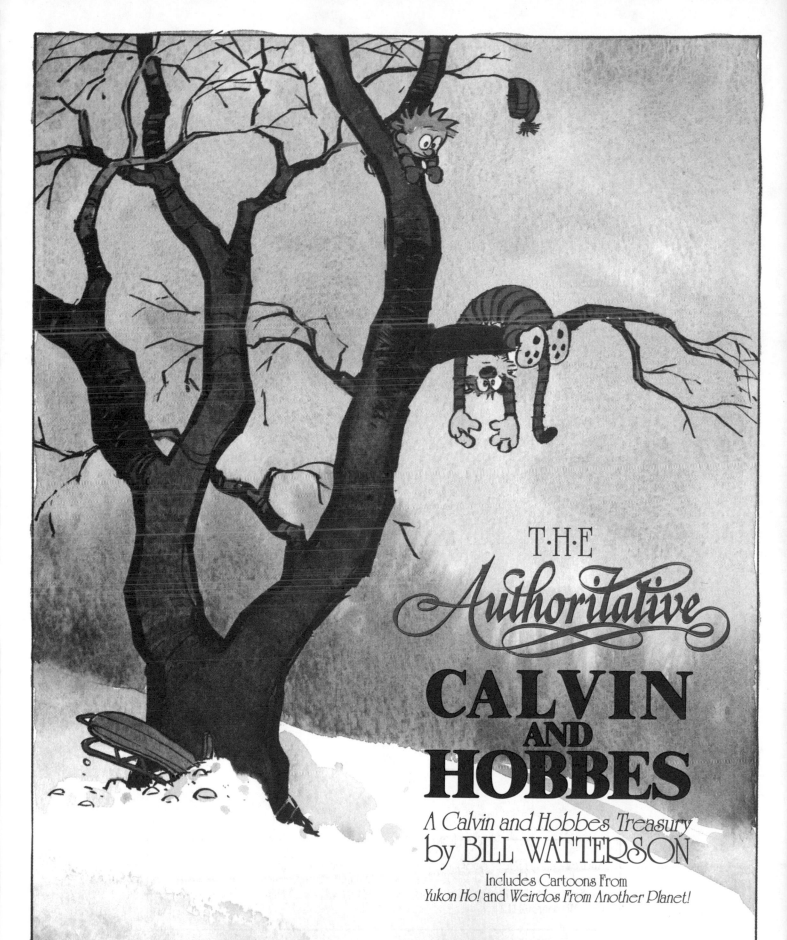

# T·H·E
# *Authoritative*
# CALVIN
# AND
# HOBBES

*A Calvin and Hobbes Treasury*
by BILL WATTERSON

Includes Cartoons From
*Yukon Ho!* and *Weirdos From Another Planet!*

Andrews and McMeel   A Universal Press Syndicate Company   Kansas City • New York

ISBN: O-8362-1864-7 (hardback)
      O-8362-1822-1 (paperback)
Library of Congress Catalog Card Number: 90-82675

To Doctor Dave and
Fellow Moosers John, Brad, and The Frey

# CALVIN and HOBBES
by WATERSON

ARRGH! I'M *NEVER* GOING TO BE ABLE TO MEMORIZE ALL THESE DUMB VOCABULARY WORDS!

TRANSMOG-RIFIER

ZAP

TRANSMOG-RIFIER

WUMP WUMP WUMP

HOW CAN ONE LITTLE KID MAKE SO MUCH NOISE?

CALVIN, WHAT ARE YOU DOING UP THERE?! YOU SOUND LIKE AN ELEPHANT! YOU'RE SUPPOSED TO BE DOING YOUR HOMEWORK!

CALVIN! MY, HOW YOU'VE GROWN SINCE I LAST SAW YOU!

I TRANSMOGRIFIED MYSELF TO FINISH MY HOMEWORK FASTER.

C'MON, LET'S FIND A MUD HOLE TO PLAY IN! ELEPHANTS LOVE MUD!

GREAT! YOU CAN TELL ME SOME ELEPHANT JOKES THERE!

HI CALVIN. BOY, LOOK AT YOU!

IMPRESSIVE, EH? HOW DID YOU EVEN RECOGNIZE ME?

I'LL ADMIT IT WASN'T EASY.

HEY, HERE'S A RIDDLE HOBBES MADE UP. WHO DO HOBBES AND I LOOK LIKE? CAN YOU GUESS?

I GIVE UP.

THE REPUBLICAN PARTY AND TAMMANY HALL! SEE? PRETTY GOOD, HUH? HA HA HA HA!

FORGET IT, HOBBES. POLITICAL HUMOR IS JUST TOO SOPHISTICATED FOR GIRLS.

HMPH. HER LOSS!

17

# Calvin and Hobbes
### by Watterson

"BEFORE BEGINNING ANY HOME-PLUMBING REPAIR, MAKE SURE YOU POSSESS THE PROPER TOOLS FOR THE JOB."

"CHECK THE FOLLOWING LIST OF HANDY EXPLETIVES, AND SEE THAT YOU KNOW HOW TO USE THEM."

CALVIN WAKES UP ONE MORNING TO FIND HE NO LONGER EXISTS IN THE THIRD DIMENSION! HE IS 2-D!

THINNER THAN A SHEET OF PAPER, CALVIN HAS NO SURFACE AREA ON THE BOTTOM OF HIS FEET! HE IS IMMOBILE!

ONLY BY "WAVING" HIS BODY CAN CALVIN CREATE ENOUGH FRICTION WITH THE GROUND TO MOVE!

HAVING WIDTH BUT NO THICKNESS, CALVIN IS VULNERABLE TO THE SLIGHTEST GUST OF WIND!

TO AVOID DRAFTS, HE TWISTS HIMSELF INTO A TUBE, AND ROLLS ACROSS THE FLOOR!

SOMEONE IS COMING! CALVIN QUICKLY STANDS UP STRAIGHT.

TURNING PERFECTLY SIDEWAYS, HE IS A NEARLY INVISIBLE VERTICAL LINE! NO ONE WILL NOTICE!

HEY DAD, KNOW WHY YOU DIDN'T SEE ME ALL MORNING?? I WAS TWO-DIMENSIONAL!

HMMM, I'LL BET YOU CAN'T DO IT ALL AFTERNOON, TOO...

DEAR!

I COULDN'T READ IT BECAUSE MY PARENTS FORGOT TO PAY THE GRAVITY BILL.

MAKE A PREDICTION, HOBBES. WHAT FOR?

SO WE CAN SEE IF YOU HAVE ESP.

OK, I PREDICT YOU'LL FIND AN IRRESISTIBLE ATTRACTION TO A MUD HOLE.

HA HA. YOU STAY AWAY FROM ME. IT'S GOING TO COME TRUE! I CAN FEEL IT!

HEY DAD, HOW DOES A CARBURETOR WORK?

I CAN'T TELL YOU.

WHY NOT?

IT'S A SECRET. NO IT ISN'T! YOU JUST DON'T KNOW!

19

BOMBARDED BY HIGH-ENERGY PHOTONS, CALVIN IS TRANSFORMED INTO A LIVING X-RAY!

ALTHOUGH THIS CONDITION WILL FACILITATE FUTURE MEDICAL DIAGNOSES, IT DOES MAKE CALVIN'S PRESENCE AT THE DINNER TABLE A DISGUSTING ORDEAL!

EVERYONE CAN SEE CALVIN'S FOOD BEING GROUND INTO MUSHY PULP AND SWALLOWED! AT THIS MOMENT, CALVIN CHEWS UP A LARGE SPOONFUL OF CREAMED CORN!

FOR GOSH SAKES, CLOSE YOUR MOUTH WHEN YOU CHEW!! YOU THINK WE WANT TO *SEE* THAT?!

MKGHH! SMACK! BLAGHKH!

HERE'S A LITTLE TOWN.

HERE'S A STEAMSHOVEL SCOOPING OUT A GIANT HOLE.

HERE COMES THE BULLDOZER, PUSHING THOUSANDS OF BARRELS OF TOXIC NUCLEAR WASTE INTO THE GIANT HOLE.

OVER THE YEARS, THESE DANGEROUS POISONS SEEP INTO UNDERGROUND WATERWAYS.

THE CANCER RATE OF THE NEARBY LITTLE TOWN TRIPLES.

IF YOU WANT ME, I'LL BE UNDER THE BED.

**A STRIKE?!** THAT PITCH WAS FOUR FEET ABOVE MY HEAD!

HA! IT WAS A *PERFECT* PITCH! YOU'RE JUST TOO SHORT!

YEAH? WELL, *YOU'RE* JUST TOO STUPID!

WELL, YOU'RE JUST TOO *UGLY!*

KICK KICK KICK KICK

KICK KICK KICK KICK KICK

KICKING DUST IS THE ONLY PART OF THIS GAME WE REALLY LIKE.

# Calvin and Hobbes

by WATTERSON

"I'M GOING OUTSIDE, MOM!"

"HOLD ALL MY CALLS."

"CALVIN LOOKS AROUND. SOMETHING IS DIFFERENT."

"THE ODD-COLORED TREE BEHIND HIM SLOWLY LIFTS UP! IT'S NOT A TREE AT ALL! IT'S A LEG!"

"OH NO! CALVIN IS THE SIZE OF A BUG *TO* A BUG! HE RUNS FOR HIS LIFE!"

"A CLAW CRASHES WITH DEAFENING IMPACT! THE BUG IS TRYING TO STEP ON CALVIN! WHAT A HORRIBLE FATE!"

"CALVIN SCRAMBLES MADLY, PROMISING HIMSELF THAT HE'LL NEVER SQUISH ANOTHER BUG IF HE LIVES TO RETURN TO NORMAL SIZE!"

"SUDDENLY IN A SPRAY OF SLIME, THE BUG IS GONE! A MONSTROUS FROG LICKS ITS CHOPS! CALVIN IS SAVED!"

"AACCK! WHAT'S THAT ON MY PLATE?! GOOD HEAVENS, GET IT OFF THE TABLE!!"

"BUT MOM, FROGS ARE OUR *FRIENDS!*"

24

OK, I THINK THAT'S DAD'S BUILDING UP AHEAD.

I'M NOT SURE WHERE HIS OFFICE IS, SO WE'LL JUST HAVE TO LOOK IN THE WINDOWS AS WE ZIP BY.

HEY! THERE HE IS! THERE'S DAD! HI, DAD! DAD, LOOK! OUT THE WINDOW!!

DARN IT! HE'S STILL READING THAT BRIEF. LOOK OUT THE WINDOW, DAD!

DID YOU BRING ANY ROCKS? I DIDN'T THINK TO.

HEY DAD! LOOK OUT THE WINDOW! ...I CAN'T BELIEVE HE'S JUST SITTING IN THERE.

WHY DOESN'T HE LOOK UP?

I GUESS HE'S PRETTY BUSY.

YEAH, BUT WE CAN'T SIT UP HERE ALL DAY! SHEESH. LET'S GO.

IF HE HAD NOTICED US, WE COULD'VE GIVEN HIM A RIDE HOME.

HMPH. I SAY LET HIM TAKE THE SMELLY OL' BUS IF HE CAN'T EVEN LOOK OUT THE WINDOW ONCE IN A WHILE. SERVES HIM RIGHT.

I'M HOME!

DAD! HOBBES AND I FLEW BY YOUR OFFICE WINDOW TODAY ON A RUG! WE SAW YOU WORKING.

WE WAVED AND HOLLERED, BUT YOU DIDN'T EVEN LOOK UP. WE COULDN'T BELIEVE IT. YOU MISSED THE WHOLE THING!

I THOUGHT WE WERE CUTTING DOWN HIS SUGAR INTAKE.

# Calvin and Hobbes
by WATTERSON

OH BOY OH BOY OH BOY OH BOY OH BOY OH BOY OH BOY OH BOY OH BOY OH BOY

WAIT! WAIT! I'VE GOT TO SAVOR THIS MOMENT! THE BRILLIANCE OF IT ALL! I'M A GENIUS! A SHEER *GENIUS!*

SUSIE'S PLAYING ON THE SIDEWALK! NOW'S MY CHANCE TO USE THE SNOWBALL I'VE BEEN SAVING IN THE FREEZER!

SHE'LL NEVER EXPECT A SNOWBALL IN *JUNE!* BOY, WILL SHE BE MAD! HA HA HA!

THIS IS GOING TO BE GREAT! HERE IT COMES! OH BOY! OH BOY!

HEY SUSIE!!

PIFF

I *MISSED!* DARN IT DARN IT DARN IT!! OF ALL THE MISERABLE LUCK!

AAARRGHH!

THERE MUST'VE BEEN A CROSS BREEZE! I CAN'T BELIEVE IT! I SAVED THAT SNOWBALL FOR THREE WHOLE MONTHS! I...

SCOOP SCOOP

I.. I...UH...

POW

THE IRONY OF THIS IS JUST SICKENING.

27

**I WANNA HORSEY RIDE!**

**I'M BUSY, CALVIN.**

**YOU KNOW, DAD, IT WON'T BE LONG BEFORE I'M ALL GROWN UP. ONE DAY YOU'LL WAKE UP AND WONDER HOW ALL THE YEARS SLIPPED BY.**

**YOU'LL LOOK BACK AND SAY, "WHERE HAS THE TIME GONE? CALVIN'S SO BIG, IT'S HARD TO REMEMBER WHEN HE WAS SMALL ENOUGH THAT I COULD GIVE HIM HORSEY RIDES." ...BUT THOSE DAYS WILL BE LOST FOREVER.**

**I THINK I'VE WORKED THROUGH MY POTENTIAL GUILT NOW.**

**NO, NO! JUMP THE FENCE!**

**I READ THAT GIRLS ARE MADE OF "SUGAR AND SPICE, AND EVERYTHING NICE"...**

**...WHEREAS BOYS ARE MADE OF " SNIPS AND SNAILS, AND PUPPY DOGS' TAILS."**

**HMPH.**

**SO WHAT ARE *TIGERS* MADE OF?**

**"DRAGONFLIES AND KATYDIDS, BUT MOSTLY CHEWED-UP LITTLE KIDS."**

**OH, THAT'S CLEVER.**

**DO YOU HAVE ANY MONEY?**

**NOPE.**

**HMM... HOW CAN WE GET SOME?**

**WHO DO WE KNOW THAT WE COULD SUE?**

**Calvin and Hobbes** by WATTERSON

THE DREADED SCUM BEINGS FIRE! SPACEMAN SPIFF IS *HIT!*

IT NEVER FAILS. I JUST WASHED AND WAXED THIS THING.

OUR HERO, THE INTREPID SPACEMAN SPIFF, STRUGGLES WITH THE CONTROLS OF HIS DAMAGED SPACECRAFT!

THE FREEM PROPULSION BLASTERS ARE USELESS! SPIFF CRASHES ONTO THE SURFACE OF AN ALIEN PLANET!

UNSCATHED, THE FEARLESS SPACE EXPLORER EMERGES FROM THE SMOLDERING WRECKAGE! HE IS MAROONED ON A HOSTILE WORLD!

SCORCHED BY TWIN SUNS, THE PLANET IS NOTHING BUT BARREN ROCK AND METHANE! THERE'S NO HOPE OF FINDING FOOD OR WATER!

SPIFF COLLAPSES! OH NO, A HIDEOUS ALIEN SPOTS HIM! IN HIS WEAKENED STATE, SPIFF IS NO MATCH FOR THE MONSTER! *THIS COULD BE THE END!!*

WATTERSON

LUNCHTIME! I BROUGHT YOU A SANDWICH AND SOME LEMONADE.

BRING THE DISHES BACK WHEN YOU'RE DONE, OK?

...OH WELL.

THANKS, MOM.

QUICK, MOM! ALIENS JUST LANDED IN THE BACK YARD! THEY DEMAND TO TALK TO YOU!

YOU GO ON OUT! I'LL GUARD THE COOKIES IN THE KITCHEN!

QUICK! HURRY!

SHE'S NOT BUYING THIS.

CALVIN, JUST HOW DUMB DO YOU THINK I AM?

WHAT DO YOU THINK IS THE SECRET TO HAPPINESS? IS IT MONEY, POWER OR FAME?

*I'D* CHOOSE MONEY. IF YOU HAVE ENOUGH MONEY, YOU CAN *BUY* POWER AND FAME. THAT WAY YOU'D HAVE IT ALL AND BE *REALLY* HAPPY!

HAPPINESS IS BEING FAMOUS FOR YOUR FINANCIAL ABILITY TO INDULGE IN EVERY KIND OF EXCESS.

I SUPPOSE THAT'S *ONE* WAY TO DEFINE IT.

THE PART I THINK I'D LIKE BEST IS CRUSHING PEOPLE WHO GET IN MY WAY.

LOOK! SOMEBODY POURED NEW CEMENT!

IS ANYONE LOOKING? WE COULD WRITE OUR INITIALS IN IT, OR MAKE A HAND PRINT, OR SOMETHING!

YEAH! "OR SOMETHING"!

I THINK WE'D BETTER FIND A HOSE QUICK!

I DIDN'T THINK IT WOULD SET UP SO FAST.

# Calvin and Hobbes
### by WATTERSON

PSST... HEY, KID. C'MERE UNDER THE BED. I'VE GOT A BRAND NEW TOY FOR YOU.

UH OH. I THINK I SAW A TENTACLE UNDER THE BED!

MONSTERS!

TURN ON THE LIGHTS! THAT MAKES MONSTERS SHRIVEL UP.

GOOD IDEA.

CLICK!

AARRGHHH! AIEEEE AAHHHHHH!! GAACKK

HA HA. WE GOT 'EM!

JUST THE ONES UNDER THE BED. WE'D BETTER OPEN UP THE DRAWERS AND CLOSET TOO, AND GET SOME LIGHT IN THOSE PLACES!

BY GOLLY, NO MONSTERS ARE GOING TO GET *US* TONIGHT! WITHER AND DIE, BLOODSUCKING FREAKS OF NATURE!!

WHY IS YOUR LIGHT ON? WHAT IN THE WORLD ARE YOU *DOING*?!?

MONSTERS, DAD. THEY COULD BE ANYWHERE.

YOU'RE TRASHING YOUR ROOM AT 1:00 IN THE MORNING, LOOKING FOR *MONSTERS*?! IF YOU DON'T GET IN BED THIS *INSTANT*, YOU'LL HAVE A LOT MORE TO WORRY ABOUT THAN STUPID MONSTERS!!

..WHAT WE *NEED* IS SOME WAY TO SHRIVEL *HIM* UP.

# Calvin and Hobbes

by WATTERSON

CAN YOU BELIEVE THIS? SOME IDIOT TOSSED GARBAGE HERE IN THIS BEAUTIFUL SPOT.

I'LL BET FUTURE CIVILIZATIONS FIND OUT MORE ABOUT US THAN WE'D LIKE THEM TO KNOW.

LOOK, ANOTHER CAN THROWN ON THE GROUND! BOY, THIS MAKES ME MAD!

BY GOLLY, IF PEOPLE AREN'T BURYING TOXIC WASTES OR TESTING NUCLEAR WEAPONS, THEY'RE THROWING TRASH EVERYWHERE!

YOU'D THINK PLANETS LIKE THIS WERE A DIME A DOZEN! NOW *I'VE* GOT TO CARRY THIS GROSS THING.

YOU KNOW, THERE ARE TIMES WHEN IT'S A SOURCE OF PERSONAL PRIDE TO NOT BE HUMAN.

I'M WITH YOU.

**Calvin:** HEY MOM, WHAT'S THIS I HEAR ABOUT THE GREENHOUSE EFFECT?

**Mom:** THEY SAY THE POLLUTANTS WE DUMP IN THE AIR ARE TRAPPING IN THE SUN'S HEAT AND IT'S GOING TO MELT THE POLAR ICE CAPS!

**Calvin:** SURE, *YOU'LL* BE GONE WHEN IT HAPPENS, BUT *I* WON'T! NICE PLANET YOU'RE LEAVING ME!

**Mom:** THIS FROM THE KID WHO WANTS TO BE CHAUFFEURED ANY PLACE MORE THAN A BLOCK AWAY.

**Calvin:** HEY, NOBODY TOLD ME ABOUT THE ICE CAPS, ALL RIGHT?

**Calvin:** MORE BAD NEWS ON YOUR POLLS, DAD. WE'RE LOOKING AT AN ALL-TIME LOW IN POPULARITY HERE.

**Dad:** WELL, CALVIN, THAT'S CERTAINLY FOOD FOR THOUGHT.

**Dad:** NOW HERE'S SOMETHING *YOU* CAN THINK ABOUT. THE AVERAGE COST OF RAISING A KID TO AGE 18 IS $100,000. THAT'S A LOT OF MONEY.

**Dad:** SO THE QUESTION YOU SHOULD BE ASKING YOURSELF IS, "IS THAT HUNDRED GRAND A *GIFT*... OR A *LOAN?*"

**Calvin:** GOTCHA, DAD. I WAS JUST ON MY WAY TO BED.

RING RING

**Calvin:** HELLO?

**Caller:** MAY I SPEAK WITH YOUR FATHER, PLEASE?

**Calvin:** HECK, YOU DON'T NEED *MY* PERMISSION! BE MY GUEST!

**Calvin:** WHAT A WEIRDO.

RING RING

DEEP IN A DANK DUNGEON ON THE DISMAL PLANET ZOG, THE FEARLESS SPACEMAN SPIFF IS HELD PRISONER BY THE SINISTER ZOG KING.

A GUARD LEADS SPIFF TO THE INTERROGATION ROOM. OUR HERO IS STOIC AND DEFIANT!

AT LAST I MEET THE FAMED SPACEMAN SPIFF! I TRUST YOU ARE...HEH HEH... ENJOYING YOUR VISIT?

YOU'RE WASTING YOUR TIME, MAGGOT FROM MARS! I'LL NEVER GIVE IN!

NEVER, YOU HEAR ME?! NEVER!

KID, DON'T MAKE ME RECANT THE HIPPOCRATIC OATH, OK?

WELL, YOU CERTAINLY WERE A TERROR IN THE DOCTOR'S OFFICE.

I FENDED HIM OFF WITH HIS OWN TONGUE DEPRESSOR. THAT'S WHY I DIDN'T GET A SHOT.

YOU DIDN'T NEED A SHOT. YOUR BEHAVIOR WAS INEXCUSABLE.

ALL THAT COUNTS IS THAT HE COULDN'T GET NEAR ENOUGH TO STICK ME. HE THINKS I'M A LITTLE PINK PIN CUSHION IN UNDERPANTS.

SOMEDAY I HOPE YOU HAVE A KID THAT PUTS YOU THROUGH WHAT I'VE GONE THROUGH.

YEAH, GRANDMA SAYS THAT'S WHAT SHE USED TO TELL YOU.

HERE IS A PROUD CITY, FULL OF HAPPY, PROSPEROUS CITIZENS.

THEY GO ON ABOUT THEIR BUSINESS, UNAWARE THAT THE MOON HAS MYSTERIOUSLY MOVED A FEW MILES CLOSER TO THE EARTH.

...UNAWARE, THAT IS, UNTIL THE TIDE COMES IN.

SPLOOSH!
GISSHHH!

# Calvin and Hobbes
by WATTERSON

THE FIRE'S NOT LIGHTING, HUH? CAN I MAKE A SUGGESTION?

GIVE UP ON THAT SISSY LIGHTER FLUID.

CAN'T WE COOK THE HAMBURGERS YET?

THE COALS AREN'T HOT ENOUGH.

BUT I'M HUNGRY! I WANT TO EAT *NOW!*

WELL, YOU'LL JUST HAVE TO WAIT.

YOU KNOW, CALVIN, SOMETIMES THE ANTICIPATION OF SOMETHING IS MORE FUN THAN THE THING ITSELF ONCE YOU GET IT.

HERE WE ARE, IT'S A BEAUTIFUL EVENING. IT'S NICE TO JUST SIT HERE AND LOOK AT THE TREES WHILE WE WAIT FOR THE COALS TO GET HOT, DON'T YOU THINK?

DINNER WILL BE OVER SOON, AND AFTERWARD WE'LL BE DISTRACTED WITH OTHER THINGS TO DO. BUT NOW WE HAVE A FEW MINUTES TO OURSELVES TO ENJOY THE EVENING.

THESE SUMMER DAYS GO BY SO QUICKLY. IT'S GOOD THAT EVERY NOW AND THEN WE HAVE TO WAIT FOR SOMETHING.

SO SHOULD I GO TO McDONALD'S THEN, OR WHAT?

YEAH, I KNOW. YOU THINK YOU'RE GOING TO BE SIX ALL YOUR LIFE.

WHAT A PERFECT DAY!

ISN'T IT GREAT TO BE ON SUMMER VACATION? TO BE ABLE TO ENJOY ALL THIS WITH NO SCHOOL AND NO RESPONSIBILITIES?

..AHHHHHHH...

I CAN'T BELIEVE THERE'S NOTHING ON TV BUT REPEATS.

I THINK A BEE LANDED ON MY BACK! CAN YOU SEE IT? I DON'T WANT TO MOVE!

THAT'S NOT A BEE.

IT ISN'T?
*WHEW*

NO, THAT'S A HORNET IF I EVER SAW ONE!

OW!

46

# Calvin and Hobbes

by WATTERSON

**WIPE THAT GRIN OFF YOUR FACE!**

**WELL, HOBBES, HOW DO I LOOK?**

**I'M DOING MY BEST TO BITE MY TONGUE.**

**I CUT OUT CONSTRUCTION PAPER FEATHERS AND TAPED THEM ON MY ARMS SO I CAN FLY! PRETTY NEAT, HUH?**

**IF PAPER FEATHERS ARE ALL IT TAKES TO FLY, DON'T YOU THINK WE'D HAVE HEARD ABOUT IT BEFORE?**

**IT TAKES AN UNCOMMON MIND TO THINK OF THESE THINGS, HOBBES.**

**I'D AGREE WITH THAT.**

**HERE'S A GORGE. THIS IS A GOOD SPOT.**

**YOU'RE GOING TO JUMP OFF THIS LEDGE?**

**HECK NO! I NEED MOMENTUM! I WANT YOU TO TOSS ME OVER.**

**YOU UNDERSTAND I ASSUME NO RESPONSIBILITY FOR THIS?**

**RIGHT. I GET THE PATENT.**

**HEAVE!**

**I'M FLYING! I'M FLYING!**

**I'M..... UH OH...**

**DON'T SELL THE BIKE SHOP, ORVILLE.**

**SHUT UP AND GO GET ME SOME ANTISEPTIC.**

# Calvin and Hobbes
by WATTERSON

THAT RUN DOESN'T COUNT! YOU DIDN'T TOUCH THIRD BASE!

THAT'S 'CAUSE THIRD BASE CRAWLED TO THE OUTFIELD!

WAP!

HA HA! EASY OUT!!

HEY! WHERE ARE YOU GOING?!

EEEEEEE

YOU HAVE TO STAY ON THE BASE LINE, YOU CHEATER!

YEAH? PROVE IT!

THIS ISN'T FAIR! YOU CAN'T RUN ANYWHERE!

JUST WATCH ME!

IF WE HAD A FIRST BASE MAN, YOU'D'VE BEEN OUT LONG AGO!

BUT WE DON'T, DO WE?

GOTCHA! YOU'RE OUT!

OK, I'M UP TO BAT AGAIN! WHAT FUN! TWO-MAN BASEBALL IS A REAL SPORT!

A REAL SPORT FOR IDIOTS. NEXT TIME I'M GOING TO TAG YOU OUT WITH THE BAT INSTEAD OF THE BALL.

48

49

TUM DE TA TA DEE DEE DO

BOY, THIS SURE BEATS SITTING IN AN OFFICE ALL DAY!

IS IT STILL RAINING?

OF COURSE IT'S STILL RAINING. IT'S BEEN RAINING FOR DAYS. WHY SHOULD IT STOP NOW?!

WE'RE GOING TO NEED A VACATION AFTER *THIS* VACATION.

I'LL SAY! WE CAN'T EVEN KEEP A FIRE GOING.

I CAN'T BELIEVE DAD WENT OUT TO CATCH FISH.

IN *THIS* WEATHER? HE'S A FANATIC!

EITHER THAT, OR WE'RE ALL OUT OF PACKAGED FOOD. WE'LL PROBABLY STARVE TO DEATH ON THIS GOD-FORSAKEN ROCK.

AFTER ALL THAT SPAM, STARVING DOESN'T SOUND SO BAD.

IF WE LIVE TO GET HOME, I'M NEVER GOING TO SET FOOT OUTSIDE AGAIN AS LONG AS I LIVE.

WHAT A LUCKY KID CALVIN IS! I NEVER GOT TO DO THIS STUFF WHEN *I* WAS HIS AGE!

HEY CALVIN! WANT TO LEARN HOW TO GUT A FISH?

WELL, GANG, I'M SORRY THE WEATHER WASN'T ANY BETTER THIS WEEK.

I KNOW IT WASN'T ALWAYS A LOT OF FUN, BUT WE LIVED THROUGH IT, AND WE GOT TO SPEND SOME TIME TOGETHER, AND THAT'S WHAT'S REALLY IMPORTANT.

ANYWAY, I HOPE YOU'RE ALL NOT *TOO* DISAPPOINTED.

CALVIN, TELL YOUR DAD ANY JUDGE WOULD TAKE THIS TRIP AS GROUNDS FOR DIVORCE.

DAD, MOM SAYS...

ALL RIGHT! ALL RIGHT!

DAD, CAN YOU GET MY BALL OUT OF THE GUTTER AGAIN?

THIS IS THE THIRD TIME THIS AFTERNOON! I THOUGHT I TOLD YOU TO PLAY OUT BACK!

RELAX, DAD. IT'S JUST A BALL IN THE GUTTER. IT'S NOT AS IF I'VE BEEN EMBEZZLING MONEY OR KILLING PEOPLE, RIGHT? AREN'T YOU GLAD I'M NOT STEALING AND MURDERING?

I ALWAYS HAVE TO HELP DAD ESTABLISH THE PROPER CONTEXT.

C'MON, HOBBES. LET DOWN THE ROPE LADDER.

WHAT'S THE REST OF THE PASSWORD?

I THINK FIVE VERSES EXTOLLING TIGERS IS *PLENTY*. YOU KNOW IT'S ME! LET ME UP!

NO.

OOH, WHY YOU LOUSY, ROTTEN, STINKING..

IF YOU CALL ME NAMES, YOU HAVE TO START OVER AT THE BEGINNING.

VERSE SIX: "TIGERS ARE NIMBLE AND LIGHT ON THEIR TOES, MY *RE*SPECT FOR TIGERS CONTINUALLY GROWS."

YOU'RE NOT DOING THE DANCE.

# Calvin and Hobbes by WATTERSON

AH-CHOO!

*WHEW* ... NO BRAINS.

AH.. AH.. AH.. **AH**

CHOOO!

THE FORCE OF THE NASAL EXPLOSION SENDS CALVIN REELING THROUGH THE STRATOSPHERE!

WITH LESS AND LESS AIR TO RESIST HIS MOMENTUM, HE BREAKS THE PULL OF EARTH'S GRAVITY AND HURLS PAST THE MOON!

AS HE PASSES OUT OF THE GALAXY, CALVIN REFLECTS ON THE WISDOM OF COVERING ONE'S MOUTH WHEN SNEEZING TO DEFLECT THE PROPULSION.

ALAS, IT IS KNOWLEDGE GAINED TOO LATE FOR POOR CALVIN, THE HUMAN SATELLITE! ...BUT WAIT! ANOTHER SNEEZE IS BREWING! CALVIN TURNS HIMSELF AROUND!

THE SECOND SNEEZE ROCKETS HIM BACK TO EARTH! HE'S SAVED! IT'S A MIRACLE!

AH CHOO!

GOD BLESS YOU.

OH, HE *DOES*, MOM. HE *DOES*.

RATS. I CAN'T TELL MY GUM FROM MY SILLY PUTTY.

WAP WAP WAP WAP

WIPPITY WAPPITY WIPPITY WAPPITY

BIPPITABIPPITABIPPITABIPPITABIPPITA

I'M NEVER GONNA GET MARRIED. ARE YOU?

HMM... I SUPPOSE IF THE RIGHT PERSON CAME ALONG, I MIGHT.

SOMEBODY WITH GREEN EYES AND A NICE LAUGH, WHO I COULD CALL "POOTY PIE."

"POOTY PIE"?!?

OR "BITSY POOKUMS."

I THINK THAT WOULD AFFECT MY STOMACH A LOT MORE THAN MY HEART.

"BITSY POOKUMS," I'D SAY. "YES, SNOOGY WOOGY," SHE'D REPLY...

# calvin and hobbes

by WATTERSON

STIR STIR · STRETTCCHHH · STAB STAB · PAT PAT PAT · MUSH MUSH · SNIFF

HWOOF! · LICK · ACKPTGH · BLECHH · GLUG GLUG GLUG · SMACK · BR-R-R-R-R

HAAAKK HOCCHH

CHOKE... GASP...

THERE...(PANT)... SEE? I...I...**TRIED** IT. (COUGH) IT... ALMOST (WHEEZE) KILLED... ME.

CLAP CLAP CLAP CLAP CL

ENCORE.

BRA**VO**.

I'M GOING TO RUN AWAY TO ALASKA.

WATTERSON

WANT TO GO TIME TRAVELING WITH ME?

SEE, I BUILT A TIME MACHINE.

TIME MACHINE

THIS LOOKS LIKE YOUR TRANSMOGRIFIER.

TO THE INATTENTIVE AND BRAINLESS LAYMAN, YES. BUT YOU CRAWL UNDER THE TRANSMOGRIFIER, WHEREAS WITH THE TIME MACHINE, YOU CLIMB IN THE TOP.

AHH..

ARE WE GOING TO TRAVEL INTO THE PAST OR INTO THE FUTURE?

WELL, I SUPPOSE IF WE WENT INTO THE PAST, I COULD ACE ANY UPCOMING HISTORY EXAMS IN SCHOOL. THAT MIGHT BE USEFUL.

BUT IF WE WENT INTO THE FUTURE, WE COULD SWIPE SOMETHING AND PRETEND TO INVENT IT WHEN WE GOT BACK. WE COULD BE RICH.

THE FUTURE IT IS, THEN!

RIGHT. ONCE I'M RICH, I CAN HIRE SOMEBODY TO TAKE ALL MY DUMB TESTS!

TIME MACHINE

OK, HOBBES, OUR TIME MACHINE IS ALL SET. PUT ON YOUR GOGGLES AND WE'LL BE OFF TO THE FUTURE!

TIME MACHINE

WHY DO WE HAVE TO WEAR GOGGLES?

GEEZ, DO YOU THINK TRAVELING YEARS INTO THE FUTURE IS LIKE DRIVING DOWN THE STREET?!

WE'VE GOT TO CONTEND WITH VORTEXES AND LIGHT SPEEDS! ANYTHING COULD GO WRONG! OF COURSE WE NEED TO WEAR GOGGLES!

GOSH, I THINK MY GOGGLES ARE IN THE BEDROOM. IF I'M NOT BACK IN A COUPLE MINUTES, YOU CAN GO WITHOUT ME.

SIT DOWN, SISSY. I ALREADY GOT YOUR GOGGLES.

TIME MACHINE

LET'S HAVE A LOOK AROUND. I'M SURE WE'LL RUN INTO A ROBOT OR SOMETHING.

TIME MACHINE

LOOK AT THIS.

GOSH, I WONDER WHAT FUTURISTIC DEVICE THIS IS! SOME SORT OF TRANSPORTATION POD, I'D GUESS.

I WONDER HOW YOU GET IN?

I DON'T SEE A DOOR OR LICENSE NUMBER ANYWHERE.

THIS IS VERY PECULIAR.

HAVE YOU EVER SEEN A TREE THIS COLOR?

---

I MUST SAY, THE FUTURE IS QUITE A BIT DIFFERENT THAN I EXPECTED.

THIS BREEZE IS SO HOT AND MUGGY. I FIGURED THEY'D BE ABLE TO CONTROL THE WEATHER BY NOW.

THE AIR STINKS, TOO. I GUESS THERE'S STILL POLLUTION.

EVER FEEL AS IF YOU'RE BEING MONITORED?

..OR THAT YOU'RE ABOUT TO DO A DOUBLE-TAKE?

---

AAUGH BACK TO THE TIME MACHINE! RUN!

WE MUST'VE GONE BACK IN TIME INSTEAD OF FORWARD!

WHAT TIPPED YOU OFF? THE DINOSAUR?!

DON'T GET SMART, FUZZBRAIN. JUST GET IN AND FACE THE OTHER DIRECTION SO WE GO INTO THE FUTURE THIS TIME!

YOU MEAN WE WENT INTO THE PAST BECAUSE WE WERE FACING THE WRONG WAY?!?

YOU THINK I'VE GOT SOME TRIPLE-A MAP?! MAYBE YOU'D LIKE TO STEER THIS TIME!

IF YOU COULD HAVE THREE WISHES GRANTED, WHAT WOULD THEY BE?

JUST THREE WISHES, HUH? HMM... THAT WOULD BE A TOUGH DECISION.

I GUESS I'D HAVE TO THINK ABOUT IT A WHILE.

OOPS! HANG ON.

OK, I KNOW WHAT MY FIRST WISH WOULD BE.

ONE OF NATURE'S UGLIER CREATURES, THE BAT IS A MISUNDERSTOOD MARVEL OF EVOLUTION.

PRODUCING A SERIES OF LOUD, HIGH-PITCHED SQUEAKS, THE BAT CAN JUDGE AN INSECT'S DISTANCE AND ELEVATION BY THE TIME DELAY OF THE SQUEAK'S ECHO!

CHANGES IN THE ECHO'S PITCH REVEAL THE DOOMED BUG'S DIRECTION! NO MOVEMENT ESCAPES THE INCREDIBLE SENSES OF THE BAT!

GLUMP!
TA-DAA! EYES CLOSED!

CALVIN, SIT UP AND EAT WITH A FORK LIKE A CIVILIZED HUMAN BEING.

YAWN

WAAUUGHH!

FOR THE LAST TIME, GET OUT OF BED! WE'RE GOING TO BE LATE.

I'M TRYING. I'M TRYING.

WELL, I GUESS WE'RE ALL PACKED. COMIC BOOKS, DART GUN, SPACE HELMET AND TOBOGGAN! WE'RE OFF TO THE YUKON!

DO WE HAVE A MAP?

OOH, THAT'S RIGHT! GLAD YOU REMEMBERED! I'LL GO GET ONE!

DON'T WE HAVE ANY ROAD MAPS OF THE YUKON, MOM?

I DOUBT IT.

OK, HERE'S THE YUKON. NOW SEE IF YOU CAN FIND THE UNITED STATES.

HERE THEY ARE! LOOK HOW CLOSE IT IS! THIS WON'T TAKE ANY TIME AT ALL!

SO LONG, "MOM"! WE'RE OFF TO THE YUKON. IT'S BEEN NICE LIVING HERE ... BUT NOT REAL NICE! HA HA!

CALVIN! WAIT A MINUTE.

LEAVE IT TO A MOTHER TO DRAG OUT A GOODBYE. SHEESH.

YOU'RE GOING SOUTHEAST. NORTH IS THAT WAY.

OH YEAH. I KNEW THAT.

THIS SLED IS HEAVY. I THOUGHT WE WERE GOING TO RIDE IT MOST OF THE WAY TO THE YUKON.

WE'VE ONLY BEEN WALKING 20 MINUTES, HOBBES. WE PROBABLY WON'T GET TO NORTHERN CANADA UNTIL THIS AFTERNOON.

IN THAT CASE, I'M TAKING A BREAK.

GOOD IDEA. WANT A COMIC BOOK? HERE'S CAPTAIN NITRO.

I WANT A SANDWICH.

WE JUST HAVE ONE APIECE. WE SHOULD SAVE 'EM IN CASE WE CAN'T CATCH A WALRUS.

# Calvin and Hobbes
### by WATTERSON

HOBBES, YOU MANGY FUZZ-BRAINED LUNKHEAD, WHERE ARE YOU??

...I DIDN'T MEAN THAT QUITE THE WAY THAT SOUNDED.

C'MON, CALVIN, GET BACK INSIDE. IT'S TOO LATE TO GO SEARCHING FOR YOUR STUFFED TIGER NOW.

I CAN'T LEAVE HOBBES ALONE IN THE WOODS AT NIGHT!

WELL, MAYBE YOU SHOULD HAVE THOUGHT ABOUT THAT BEFORE IT GOT DARK. THIS CAN BE A LITTLE LESSON, HMM?

I THOUGHT HE'D COME BACK BY HIMSELF. I DIDN'T THINK HE'D GET LOST!

WE'LL LOOK FOR HIM TOMORROW. NOW OFF TO BED WITH YOU.

(SNIFF) I HOPE HE'S OK. IF HE HADN'T BEEN ACTING SO STUPID I NEVER WOULD'VE LEFT HIM.

I SURE WISH HE'D COME BACK.

CALVIN LEFT HOBBES SOMEWHERE IN THE WOODS. THE POOR KID'S PRETTY UPSET.

I'LL BET.

I MEAN, HE'S REALLY UPSET.

I SAID I'LL BET HE IS.

REALLY UPSET.

..AHH...

WOULD MY DAD HAVE DONE THIS? OF COURSE NOT. I WAS NEVER SPOILED LIKE THIS...

# CALVIN and HOBBES

by WATTERSON

EEP!

HA HA! RIGHT HERE, KID!

HELP! HELP! THE LEAF PILE'S GOT ME!!

CRUNCH CRUNCH

THE RAKE! GOTTA GET THE RAKE!

FORGET IT, KID! YOU'RE DOOMED!

YAAHH! BACK, YOU ARBOREAL MENACE! BACK!

WHAM WHAM

SINISTER FIEND! YOU WON'T BE TRICKING OTHER INNOCENT LITTLE KIDS! I'LL SPREAD YOU ACROSS THE WHOLE YARD!

I THOUGHT YOU SAID YOU WERE GOING TO RAKE THE YARD TODAY.

I DID RAKE THE YARD. I SPENT ALL AFTERNOO--

WHERE'S CALVIN?!

# Calvin and Hobbes  by WATTERSON

UH OH, IT HAPPENED AGAIN.

CALVIN WAKES UP WITHOUT ANY RECOGNIZABLE FEATURES, SAVE TWO ANTENNAE. HOW DISGUSTING.

HE OOZES OUT OF BED ON A TRAIL OF SLIME. LACKING ARMS AND LEGS, HOW WILL CALVIN PUT ON HIS CLOTHES?

AREN'T YOU DRESSED YET? YOU ARE SO SLUGGISH IN THE MORNING!

PSST...SUSIE! WHAT'S THE ANSWER TO QUESTION FOUR?

IMADOOFUS.

THANKS!

THE TOOTH FAIRY'S GONNA MAKE YOU RICH TONIGHT, SUSIE.

LET'S SEE WHAT YOU DREW FOR ART CLASS, SUSIE.

WELL, A TIDY LITTLE DOMESTIC SCENE. A HOUSE IN A YARD WITH FLOWERS. HOW TYPICALLY FEMALE.

GIRLS THINK SMALL AND ARE PREOCCUPIED WITH PETTY DETAILS. BUT *BOYS* THINK *BIG!* BOYS THINK ABOUT ACTION AND ACCOMPLISHMENT! NO WONDER IT'S *MEN* WHO CHANGE THE WORLD!

YEAH? WHAT DID *YOU* DRAW?

A SQUADRON OF B-1s NUKING NEW YORK.

MOM, CAN HOBBES AND I RENT A VCR AND A TAPE TONIGHT?

I DON'T THINK SO, CALVIN. IT'S A SCHOOL NIGHT.

WHAT IF WE GOT AN *EDUCATIONAL* TAPE?

LIKE WHAT?

"CANNIBAL STEWARDESS VIXENS UNCHAINED."

NOW SHE WON'T EVEN LET US GO INTO THE *STORE*.

I THINK WE'D LEARN A *LOT* BY WATCHING THAT.

NOBODY HAD BETTER BE SNEAKING UP ON ME !!

WHUMP!

IT'S HARD TO CHANGE DIRECTION IN MID-AIR.

BUDDY, I'M GOING TO CHANGE A LOT MORE THAN YOUR DIRECTION.

SNIP SNAP CRACK

SHICKA SHICKA WWHISSSHHH

F SHOOF SHOOF SHOOF SHO

KRITCH KRUNCH KRITCH KRUNCH

SOMETIMES IT'S GOOD TO HUSH UP A WHILE AND LET AUTUMN STICK IN A FEW WORDS.

CALVIN and HOBBES by WATTERSON

A DAZED SPACEMAN SPIFF CRAWLS FROM THE SMOKING WRECKAGE OF HIS SHIP!

OUR HERO NOW REGRETS NOT BUYING A TOWING RIDER ON HIS INSURANCE POLICY.

THE COURAGEOUS SPACE-MAN SPIFF HAS BEEN CAPTURED BY THE HIDEOUS ZORGS OF PLANET X-13!

LED THROUGH THE DANK CORRIDORS OF THE DUNGEON, SPIFF LOOKS IN VAIN FOR AN OPPORTUNITY TO ESCAPE!

OUR HERO IS BROUGHT BEFORE THE ZORG DESPOT!

SO *THIS* IS THE FAMED SPACE EXPLORER SPIFF! I'VE WAITED A LONG TIME FOR THIS MOMENT, EARTHLING SCUM!

YOU HAVE KNOWLEDGE WE NEED. COOPERATE, AND WE'LL KILL YOU RATHER PAINLESSLY.

LET'S DISPENSE WITH THE PLEASANTRIES, YOU TWISTED SPACE CRUSTACEAN. WHAT IS IT YOU WANT FROM ME?

A SUMMARY OF LEWIS AND CLARK'S EXPEDITION TO THE PACIFIC!

HA! WILD ZONTARS COULDN'T DRAG THAT INFORMATION OUT OF ME! DO YOUR WORST!

YOU DIDN'T READ THE ASSIGNMENT, DID YOU, CALVIN?

**Panel 1:** HEY, CALVIN, WHY'D YOU BRING YOUR STUFFED TIGER TO SCHOOL? IT'S NOT A SHOW AND TELL DAY.

**Panel 2:** I KNOW. HOBBES IS GOING TO GIVE MOE A LITTLE "TREAT" TODAY: A RIDE IN AN AMBULANCE HELICOPTER.

**Panel 3:** YEAH? HOW'S HE GOING TO DO *THAT*? / IF YOU HAVE AN AVERSION TO DESCRIPTIONS OF CARNAGE, YOU PROBABLY DON'T WANT TO KNOW.

**Panel 4:** TALKING WITH YOU IS SORT OF THE CONVERSATIONAL EQUIVALENT OF AN OUT-OF-BODY EXPERIENCE. / DON'T GET TOO CLOSE NOW. I WANT HOBBES TO STAY FRESH FOR THIS AFTERNOON.

**Panel 5:** LOOK, CALVIN'S GOT A TEDDY BEAR. THAT'S REAL SWEET, CAL. / IT'S A TIGER, YOU BRAINLESS INVERTEBRATE.

**Panel 6:** HEY, MAYBE I'D LIKE TO PLAY WITH YOUR TEDDY! / GOOD IDEA, MOE, HOBBES PLAYS KINDA ROUGH, BUT HE'S *LOTS* OF FUN. C'MERE AND TAKE HIM.

**Panel 7:** WHY? IS THE TEACHER WATCHING? THIS IS A TRICK, RIGHT? I'M NOT TOUCHING YOUR STUPID TEDDY, SEE? / C'MON, I DARE YOU! WHAT'S THE MATTER? ARE YOU CHICKEN?

**Panel 8:** HA HA! BOY, YOU SURE SCARED *HIM* OFF! YOU WERE GREAT! / COME BACK AND CALL ME A "BEAR" AGAIN! YEAH, *YOU*, BUB!!

**Panel 9:** I CALLED YOUR TEACHER ABOUT MOE'S BULLYING, AND SHE SAID SHE'D PUT A STOP TO IT.

**Panel 10:** I'M AFRAID YOU WASTED YOUR TIME, MOM. MOE TOOK ONE LOOK AT HOBBES AND JUST ABOUT LOST HIS LUNCH!

**Panel 11:** I DON'T THINK MOE WILL BE BOTHERING *ME* FOR A WHILE. IT'S NOT EVERY KID WHO HAS A *TIGER* FOR A BEST FRIEND.

**Panel 12:** ...AND WHAT LUCKY MOMS THOSE OTHER KIDS HAVE. / C'MON, HOBBES, IF YOU'LL LEND ME A BUCK, I'LL BUY YOU A COMIC BOOK.

PROCESSED LUNCH MEAT IS PRETTY SCARY. WHAT **ARE** THESE LITTLE SPECKS, ANYWAY? LIZARD PARTS? WHO KNOWS?

AND THIS "SKIN." I HEARD IT USED TO BE MADE OF INTESTINE, BUT I THINK NOWADAYS IT'S PLASTIC.

OF COURSE, THEY DYE AND WAX FRUIT SO IT LOOKS BETTER. IT'S LIKE EATING A CANDLE.

AND MOM WONDERS WHY I'M SO HUNGRY AFTER SCHOOL.

YEP, WE'D PROBABLY BE DEAD NOW IF IT WASN'T FOR TWINKIES.

HEY, DAD, YOUR LATEST POLL JUST CAME IN. LET'S SEE WHAT IT SAYS.

BE STILL, MY HEART.

WELL, I'LL BE! YOUR POPULARITY IS IMPROVING! YOU WENT UP 30 POINTS!

REALLY?

HECK, NO WONDER! I'M READING THE GRAPH UPSIDE-DOWN. WHAT A KLUTZ I AM!

...HOPE YOU'RE ALL PACKED, DAD.

DON'T YOU HAVE SOME HOMEWORK TO DO?

Z

Z

SNIFF SNIFF

I LIKE TO MESS WITH HIS DREAMS.

ZZ...COOKIES? FOR ME? WHY SURE, BACK UP THE TRUCK... ZZZZ

# Calvin and Hobbes

by WATERSON

YOUR DAD'S WORKING, SO TRY NOT TO BOTHER HIM, OK?

DAD, I HAVE A QUESTION.

YES?

DO PEOPLE EVER SPONTANEOUSLY COMBUST?

UH... NOT THAT I KNOW OF, NO.

THAT'S A RELIEF. THANKS, DAD.

YOU'RE WELCOME.

POW!

DID I FOOL YOU?

IF YOU'RE HAVING TROUBLE THINKING OF WAYS TO MAKE YOURSELF USEFUL, I'LL GIVE YOU SOME SUGGESTIONS.

THINK IT'S GETTING ANY COLDER OUT?

NOT REALLY.

I DON'T THINK IT'S GONNA CHANGE.

ME EITHER.

NUTS. WELL, LET'S GO IN.

WHATCHA DOIN'?

COUNTERFEITING MONEY.

IT'S REALLY HARD. LOOK AT ALL THE LITTLE LINES ON THIS BILL.

THINK ANYONE WILL FALL FOR YOUR FORGERY?

SURE. EVERYONE WILL.

OL' GEORGE HAS THE GOUT, I SEE.

I *SAID* THIS WAS HARD.

THE GIANT WHALE SWIMS TOWARD THE SURFACE!

ITS MASSIVE TAIL PUMPING FURIOUSLY, HE GAINS TERRIFYING MOMENTUM!

THE 35-TON BEHEMOTH BREACHES! HE CRASHES INTO THE SURF WITH DEAFENING IMPACT!

CALVIN, YOU'D BETTER NOT BE SPLASHING THE FLOOR, YOU HEAR ME?!

YAAAAH

STIR
STIR
STIR

I WON'T EAT ANY CEREAL THAT DOESN'T TURN THE MILK PURPLE.

THE DEADLY TORNADO MAKES ITS WAY ACROSS THE COMMUNITY!

THE CIRCLING UPDRAFT CLOCKS AT OVER 200 MPH! THE TWISTER SEARCHES FOR A TRAILER PARK!

FINDING ONE, IT TOUCHES DOWN! DEBRIS IS THROWN FOR MILES IN THE ENSUING EXPLOSION OF RUSHING AIR!

WHEN ARE YOU GOING TO CLEAN UP THIS ROOM?! IT LOOKS LIKE A...

TORNADO HIT IT, I KNOW.

OH BOY, IT'S SATURDAY!!

WHAT'S GOING ON? WHY AREN'T THERE ANY CARTOONS ON TV? IT'S JUST A TEST PATTERN.

THE TV GUIDE SAYS THEY DON'T START UNTIL 6:30.

HECK, THAT'S 45 MINUTES FROM NOW! WELL, C'MON, I'LL RACE YOU UP AND DOWN THE STAIRS!

WHY CAN'T HE EVER GET UP LIKE THIS ON SCHOOL DAYS?

GO BREAK HIS LITTLE LEGS, WILL YOU, HONEY?

BANG!

BONK

# Calvin and Hobbes
by WATTERSON

BAD NEWS ON YOUR CAMPAIGN TO STAY DAD, DAD.

OH?

YEP. THE LATEST POLL OF SIX-YEAR-OLDS IN THIS HOUSEHOLD SHOWS THAT THEY DON'T CARE ABOUT ISSUES THIS YEAR. IT'S CHARACTER THAT COUNTS.

SO WHY IS THAT BAD NEWS?

WHO'S THE BIMBO WITH YOU IN THIS OLD PROM PICTURE?

THAT "BIMBO" IS YOUR *MOTHER!*

*WHO'S* A BIMBO??

PRETTY FUNKY HAIRDO, MOM!

IT'S THE SAD TRUTH, DAD. NOBODY CARES ABOUT YOUR POSITIONS ON FATHERHOOD. WE JUST WANT TO KNOW ABOUT YOUR CHARACTER.

IF YOU'RE GOING TO BE DAD HERE, WE HAVE TO KNOW YOU'VE NEVER DONE OR SAID ANYTHING THAT WOULD REFLECT POORLY ON YOUR JUDGMENT.

I HAVE YOUR COLLEGE YEARBOOK HERE. LET'S FLIP THROUGH IT, SHALL WE?

IS THIS YOU WITH THE KEG AND THE "PARTY NAKED" T-SHIRT?

*GIVE* ME THAAAT!

GRANDPA SAYS THE COMICS WERE A LOT BETTER YEARS AGO WHEN NEWSPAPERS PRINTED THEM BIGGER.

HE SAYS COMICS NOW ARE JUST A BUNCH OF XEROXED TALKING HEADS BECAUSE THERE'S NO SPACE TO TELL A DECENT STORY OR TO SHOW ANY ACTION.

HE THINKS PEOPLE SHOULD WRITE TO THEIR NEWSPAPERS AND COMPLAIN.

YOUR GRANDPA TAKES THE FUNNIES PRETTY SERIOUSLY.

YEAH, MOM'S LOOKING INTO NURSING HOMES.

QUIT HOGGING THE BED. YOU'RE WAY OVER ON MY SIDE.

TOUGH BEANS, FUZZ FACE.

EVER THINK ABOUT GEYSERS AND WATERFALLS? HUNDREDS OF THOUSANDS OF GALLONS OF WATER! FLOWING, SPILLING, RUSHING, GUSHING, SPLASHING!

HE REALLY FIGHTS MEAN.

SPACEMAN SPIFF FLEES THE DESPICABLE SCUM BEINGS OF PLANET Q-13!

IN A SURPRISE MANEUVER, OUR HERO TURNS TO FACE THE ADVERSARY! HIS HAND TIGHTENS AROUND THE DEATH RAY TRIGGER!

IT DOESN'T RESPOND! SPIFF REACHES FOR THE MERTILIZER BEAM, BUT IT DOESN'T WORK EITHER! NEITHER DO THE PHOSPHO BOMBS OR THE MORDO BLASTERS! NOTHING IS WORKING!!

1812! GETTYSBURG! 16 FLUID OUNCES! I BEFORE E! THOMAS EDISON!

PERHAPS SOMEONE WHO HAS BEEN *PAYING ATTENTION* CAN HELP OUT CALVIN?

Z

YAAHH!

I KEEP FORGETTING THAT FIVE OF HIS SIX ENDS ARE POINTY WHEN HE LIES LIKE THAT.

SINCE SEPTEMBER, IT'S JUST GOTTEN COLDER AND COLDER.

THERE'S LESS DAYLIGHT NOW, I'VE NOTICED, TOO.

OH NO! THIS CAN ONLY MEAN ONE THING!

THE SUN IS GOING OUT! IN A FEW MORE MONTHS EARTH WILL BE A DARK AND LIFELESS BALL OF ICE!

WELL, GEE, NOW I DON'T FEEL SO BAD ABOUT NOT SETTING UP AN IRA LAST YEAR.

DAD SAYS THE SUN ISN'T GOING OUT.

HE SAYS IT'S COLDER BECAUSE OUR HEMISPHERE IS TILTED AWAY FROM THE SUN NOW.

HE SAYS WINTER WILL BE HERE SOON.

ISN'T IT SAD HOW SOME PEOPLE'S GRIP ON THEIR LIVES IS SO PRECARIOUS THAT THEY'LL EMBRACE ANY PREPOSTEROUS DELUSION RATHER THAN FACE AN OCCASIONAL BLEAK TRUTH?

ARE YOU GOING TO LIVE THE LAST FEW MONTHS OF YOUR LIFE ANY DIFFERENTLY, NOW THAT THE SUN IS GOING OUT AND WE'RE ALL DOOMED?

NO, I'VE ALWAYS BELIEVED IN LIVING EACH DAY AS IF IT WAS MY LAST, SO I NEVER HAVE ANY REGRETS.

KIND OF INSPIRING, HUH?

IF YOU WERE SOMEONE ELSE, IT MIGHT BE.

PASS ME THAT ISSUE OF CAPTAIN NAPALM WILL YOU?

MY TEACHER SAID THE SAME THING DAD DID. THE SUN *ISN'T* GOING OUT AFTER ALL!

IT'S JUST GETTING COLDER BECAUSE WINTER'S COMING. DAD WAS RIGHT ALL ALONG!

IMAGINE OL' DAD KNOWING SOMETHING LIKE THAT!

WHAT'S THIS STORY YOU'RE GOING TO READ ME, DAD? IT DOESN'T HAVE ANY ROMANCE IN IT, DOES IT?

UH...

EDIT IT OUT IF IT DOES. I HATE ROMANCE. DOES IT HAVE ANY BORING DESCRIPTION IN IT?

WELL...

SKIP IT IF YOU SEE ANY. I LIKE MY STORIES FAST AND GRIPPING.

IT DOESN'T HAVE A MORAL, DOES IT? I HATE BEING TOLD HOW TO LIVE MY LIFE. SKIP THE MORAL, TOO, OK?

DOES HIS MAJESTY PREFER COLOR PICTURES, OR BLACK AND WHITE?

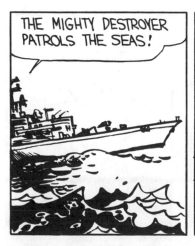

THE MIGHTY DESTROYER PATROLS THE SEAS!

SUDDENLY THE SHIP SPINS OUT OF CONTROL! IT'S CAUGHT IN A WHIRLPOOL!

WITHIN MOMENTS THE GIANT VESSEL DIPS ITS HULL INTO THE SWIRLING VORTEX AND IS NEVER SEEN AGAIN!

OH NO! HERE GOES THE REST OF THE NAVY!

ARE YOU LETTING THE WATER OUT ALREADY?

# Calvin and Hobbes

by WATTERSON

CALVIN, IT'S TIME TO WAKE UP.

CALVIN, IT'S TIME TO WAKE UP.

C'MON, YOU'LL BE LATE FOR SCHOOL.

MY DREAMS ARE GETTING WAY TOO LITERAL.

# Calvin and Hobbes by Watterson

First there was nothing...

...then there was Calvin!

Calvin, the mighty god, creates the universe with pure will!

From utter nothingness comes swirling form! Life begins where once was void!

But Calvin is no kind and loving god! He's one of the old gods! He demands sacrifice!

Yes, Calvin is a god of the underworld! And the puny inhabitants of earth displease him!

The great Calvin ignores their pleas for mercy and the doomed writhe in agony!

HAVE YOU SEEN HOW ABSORBED CALVIN IS WITH THOSE TINKERTOYS? HE'S CREATING WHOLE WORLDS OVER THERE!

I'LL BET HE GROWS UP TO BE AN ARCHITECT.

WHAT'S FOR DINNER, MOM?

TORTELLINI.

OH, NO, NOT TORTELLINI! I *HATE* TORTELLINI!! OH, GROSS! YECCH! TORTELLINI!!

NOTHING IS MORE DISGUSTING THAN TORTELLINI!! CAN'T WE HAVE SOMETHING ELSE?

NO.

TORTELLINI... TORTELLINI... T-O-R...

DID YOU SEE WE HAVE A SUBSTITUTE TEACHER TODAY?

OH, NO! THAT CAN ONLY MEAN OUR *REAL* TEACHER ROCKETED BACK TO SATURN TO REPORT TO HER SUPERIORS!

THEY'RE TRYING TO SUBVERT US LITTLE KIDS WITH SUBLIMINAL MESSAGES IN OUR TEXTBOOKS, TELLING US TO TURN IN OUR PARENTS WHEN THE SATURNIANS ATTACK! EARTH WILL BE RENDERED HELPLESS!

I THINK ONE OF US HAS BEEN EATING TOO MUCH PASTE IN ART CLASS.

I'M TOO SMART FOR 'EM, THOUGH! I DON'T READ MY ASSIGNMENTS!

BEHOLD THE TERRIBLE THUNDER LIZARD, TYRANNOSAURUS REX!

THE FIERCEST DINOSAUR OF ALL, HE IS TWENTY TONS OF BONE-CRUSHING MUSCLE AND RAZOR-SHARP TEETH!

ALWAYS THE VICTOR, HE LETS OUT A TRIUMPHANT ROAR!

BOOT

LIBRARY

AH.. **AH**.. **AH**..∘

I JUTH *HADE* IT WHED THITH HAPPEDTH.

CALVIN THE CRIMINAL IS ABOUT TO FACE JUSTICE! ANGRY THRONGS TURN OUT TO WATCH HIS EXECUTION!

AS HE IS LED UP THE GALLOWS, HE REFLECTS UPON HIS MANY HEINOUS CRIMES. HE IS NOT REPENTANT!

THE NOOSE IS PUT AROUND HIS NECK AND TIGHTENED! THIS IS THE END!

GACKK URRGHH

OH, KNOCK IT OFF. SOME OF US HAVE TO WEAR A TIE EVERY DAY.

HOW WAS THE KIDDY MATINEE MOVIE?

MOVIE? OH, YEAH, THE MOVIE. YEAH, THERE WAS A MOVIE. IT WAS OK, I GUESS.

HOW WAS THE MATINEE?

WE... ARE... BUYING... A VIDEO PLAYER.

# calvin and Hobbes

by WATTERSON

YAWN

PUTT PUTT PUTT PUTT PUTT PUTT

SCRITCH SCRATCH

RUB RUB RUB

SHOOF SHOOF SHOOF

ITCH ITCH ITCH ITCH

HMMMMM

*THAT* SIGH OUGHT TO GET ME OUT OF A FEW YEARS' PURGATORY.

# Calvin and Hobbes
## by WATTERSON

**Mom:** I DON'T KNOW, CALVIN. IT'S AWFULLY EXPENSIVE.

**Calvin:** CAN WE GET *THIS* TREE, MOM? CAN WE?

**Calvin:** YEAH, BUT JUST THINK HOW MUCH LOOT WOULD FIT UNDER IT!

**Calvin:** DAD! COME BRING IN THE CHRISTMAS TREE MOM AND I PICKED! IT'S A GREAT ONE!

**Dad:** THIS YEAR I THOUGHT WE'D JUST KEEP THE TREE IN THE GARAGE.

**Calvin:** IN THE GARAGE?!

**Dad:** SURE. YOU CAN GO OUT AND LOOK AT IT ANY TIME YOU LIKE, AND IT SAVES ALL THE TROUBLE OF DECORATING IT.

**Calvin:** WE'RE NOT GOING TO DECORATE IT?!?

**Dad:** WHY BOTHER? WE JUST TAKE IT ALL DOWN IN TWO WEEKS. ON CHRISTMAS DAY, IF YOU GET A PRESENT...

WATTERSON

**Calvin:** IF I GET A PRESENT?!

**Dad:** ...YOU CAN TAKE IT OUT TO THE GARAGE TO OPEN, AND PRETEND THE TREE HAS LOTS OF LIGHTS, AND...

**Calvin:** MOMMMM!

**Mom:** I KNOW SOMEBODY WHO'S GOING TO GET A LOT OF COAL IN HIS STOCKING, BUSTER.

**Dad:** THIS SEASON GETS LESS JOLLY EVERY YEAR.

Dear Santa,

Attached is my Christmas list for this year.

Last year I did not receive several items from my list.

For your convenience, I have grouped those items together on page 12. Please check them carefully, and include them with the rest of my loot this year.

THAT'S THE PROBLEM WITH THIS GUY. HE'S GOTTEN SLOPPY WITHOUT ANY COMPETITION.

HE SEES YOU WHEN YOU'RE SLEEPING, HE KNOWS WHEN YOU'RE AWAKE ...

HE KNOWS IF YOU'VE BEEN BAD OR GOOD, SO BE GOOD FOR GOODNESS SAKE!

* CLICK *

SANTA CLAUS: KINDLY OLD ELF, OR CIA SPOOK?

THIS SANTA CLAUS STUFF BOTHERS ME.... ESPECIALLY THE JUDGE AND JURY BIT.

WHO APPOINTED SANTA? HOW DO WE KNOW HE'S IMPARTIAL? WHAT CRITERIA DOES HE USE FOR DETERMINING GOOD AND BAD?

AND WHAT ABOUT EXTENUATING CIRCUMSTANCES? KIDS SHOULD HAVE THE BENEFIT OF LEGAL COUNSEL, DON'T YOU THINK?

YOU'RE WORRIED ABOUT THE SALAMANDER INCIDENT, AREN'T YOU?

TEMPORARY INSANITY! THAT'S ALL IT WAS!

THEY SAY SANTA KNOWS IF YOU'VE BEEN GOOD OR BAD, BUT WHAT IF SOMEONE HAD BEEN SORT OF *BOTH*?

I MEAN, SUPPOSE SOME KID *TRIED* TO BE GOOD...AT LEAST, WELL, MOST OF THE TIME...BUT BAD THINGS INEXPLICABLY KEPT HAPPENING?

SUPPOSE SOME KID JUST HAD TERRIBLE LUCK, AND HE GOT BLAMED FOR A LOT OF THINGS HE DID ONLY *SORT* OF ON PURPOSE?

WHO EXACTLY MIGHT WE BE TALKING ABOUT?

THIS IS A PURELY HYPOTHETICAL CASE, MR. SMARTY PANTS.

THIS WHOLE SANTA CLAUS THING JUST DOESN'T MAKE SENSE.

WHY ALL THE SECRECY? WHY ALL THE MYSTERY? IF THE GUY EXISTS, WHY DOESN'T HE EVER SHOW HIMSELF AND PROVE IT?

AND IF HE *DOESN'T* EXIST, WHAT'S THE MEANING OF ALL THIS?

I DUNNO... ISN'T THIS A RELIGIOUS HOLIDAY?

YEAH, BUT ACTUALLY, I'VE GOT THE SAME QUESTIONS ABOUT GOD.

GOSH, HOBBES, WHAT IF I DON'T GET ANY PRESENTS THIS YEAR BECAUSE I DOUBTED THE EXISTENCE OF SANTA?

SUPPOSE HE'S PUTTING MY NAME ON THE "BAD" LIST RIGHT NOW! THAT WOULD BE AWFUL!

PERSONALLY, I'D THINK THAT IF YOU WEREN'T ON THE "BAD" LIST ALL ALONG, THIS WOULDN'T PUSH YOU OVER.

THANKS FOR THE COMFORT, EGGNOG BRAIN.

SEE? *SEE* WHY YOU'RE ON THE "BAD" LIST? INSULTS!

**Calvin and Hobbes** by Watterson

HERE'S A BOX OF CRAYONS. I NEED SOME ILLUSTRATIONS FOR A STORY I'M WRITING.

YOU CAN DRAW SOMETHING BESIDES TIGERS, CAN'T YOU?

SURE. LEOPARDS, PUMAS, OCELOTS.. ..YOU NAME IT.

HERE, DAD, READ *THIS* STORY TONIGHT. I WROTE IT AND HOBBES ILLUSTRATED IT.

..UM... OK.

"THE DAD WHO LIVED TO REGRET BEING MEAN TO HIS KID."

WHAT ARE YOU PAUSING FOR? KEEP READING.

Barney's dad was really bad,
So Barney hatched a plan.
When his dad said, "Eat your peas!"
Barney shouted, "NO!" and ran.

peas

Barney

Barney tricked his mean ol' dad,
And locked him in the cellar.
His mom never found out
    where he'd gone,
'Cause Barney didn't tell her.

door

Key

There his dad spent his life,
Eating mice and gruel.
With every bite for fifty years
He was sorry he'd been cruel.
    THE END.

mice

Barney's dad

YOU KNOW HOW A LOT OF STORIES HAVE MORALS TO THEM...?

I *GET* IT, I *GET* IT!

WATTERSON & HOBS

I HATE WAITING FOR THE SCHOOL BUS ON DAYS LIKE THESE.

BLUSTERY COLD DAYS SHOULD BE SPENT PROPPED UP IN BED WITH A MUG OF HOT CHOCOLATE AND A PILE OF COMIC BOOKS.

THAT'S WHAT I'D LIKE TO BE DOING RIGHT NOW.

AS SOON AS I GRADUATE, I'M GOING TO SPEND *EVERY* WINTER THAT WAY.

I WISH YOUR BUS WOULD COME. MY HOT CHOCOLATE WILL GET COLD.

HELP ME FIGURE OUT THIS HOMEWORK PROBLEM, HOBBES. WHAT'S 3+8?

OK, ASSIGN THE ANSWER A VALUE OF "X". "X" ALWAYS MEANS MULTIPLY, SO TAKE THE NUMERATOR (THAT'S LATIN FOR "NUMBER EIGHTER") AND PUT THAT ON THE OTHER SIDE OF THE EQUATION.

THAT LEAVES YOU WITH THREE ON THIS SIDE, SO WHAT TIMES THREE EQUALS EIGHT? THE ANSWER, OF COURSE, IS SIX.

GOSH, I MUST HAVE DONE ALL THE OTHERS WRONG.

THESE PROBLEMS SEEM AWFULLY ADVANCED FOR FIRST GRADE, IF YOU ASK ME.

HERE'S ANOTHER MATH PROBLEM I CAN'T FIGURE OUT. WHAT'S 9+4?

OOH, THAT'S A TRICKY ONE. YOU HAVE TO USE CALCULUS AND IMAGINARY NUMBERS FOR THIS.

IMAGINARY NUMBERS?!

YOU KNOW, ELEVENTEEN, THIRTY-TWELVE, AND ALL THOSE. IT'S A LITTLE CONFUSING AT FIRST.

HOW DID *YOU* LEARN ALL THIS? YOU'VE NEVER EVEN GONE TO SCHOOL!

INSTINCT. TIGERS ARE BORN WITH IT.

IT'S FREEZING IN THIS HOUSE! SOMEBODY CRANK UP THE THERMOSTAT! WHY DOESN'T SOMEONE MAKE A FIRE?!

IF WE CAN'T AFFORD TO HEAT THIS PLACE, MAYBE DAD SHOULD GET A BETTER JOB! WHY CAN'T WE MOVE TO FLORIDA?!

CALVIN, PIPE DOWN AND PUT ON A SWEATER IF YOU'RE COLD.

AND GO TO ALL THAT TROUBLE?!

I READ THAT THE AVERAGE HOUSEHOLD WATCHES 7½ HOURS OF TV EVERY DAY.

MOM SAYS SHE DOESN'T WATCH TV AT ALL WHILE I'M AT SCHOOL...

...SO IF I GET HOME AT 3:00, I SHOULD BE ABLE TO WATCH IT STRAIGHT TILL 10:30, RIGHT?

WRONG. DO YOU WANT US TO BE SUB-AVERAGE?!

MOM, THE WASHER IS DONE.

OK.

AREN'T YOU GOING TO PUT THE WASH IN THE DRYER?

IN A MINUTE.

YOU MEAN YOU'RE JUST GOING TO LET IT SIT IN THE WASHING MACHINE?!?

CALVIN, CAN'T YOU SEE I'M BUSY RIGHT NOW??

SHE SAYS SHE'S BUSY. I HOPE THE NEXT TIME SHE TAKES A BATH THERE AREN'T ANY TOWELS.

# calvin and HOBBES by WATTERSON

TWO PARTS SLUSH...
ONE PART SOLID ICE...
ONE PART HARD-PACKED SNOW...
A DASH OF ASSORTED DEBRIS...

SCULPT INTO SPHERE, AND SERVE AT HIGH VELOCITY WITHOUT WARNING.

OH, BOY, HERE COMES SUSIE!

HEY, SUSIE!

WHAP!

HA HA! I GOTCHA, YOU DUMB GIRL!!

AUGHH!

MY EYEBALL! WHERE'S MY EYEBALL?!

WHAT ARE YOU TALKING ABOUT? I HIT YOU IN THE BACK.

IT KNOCKED MY EYEBALL OUT! FIND IT AND PACK IT IN SNOW SO THEY CAN SAVE IT! OW! OW!

GOSH, DID YOU REALLY LOSE YOUR EYEBALL? I DIDN'T KNOW THEY CAME OUT! WOW. I'M REALLY SORRY. I DIDN'T MEAN TO KNOCK IT OUT. CAN I SEE THE SOCKET? BOY, WHERE DO YOU SUPPOSE IT ROLLED?

SOMEWHERE OVER THERE, POOP HEAD!!

BOOT

WATTERSON

WHAT ARE YOU DOING?

MY EYEBALL FELL OUT. HELP ME LOOK FOR IT.

DO YOU HAVE ANY KIDS, UNCLE MAX?

ME? NOPE, I'M NOT EVEN MARRIED.

OH.

...WHAT DIFFERENCE DOES *THAT* MAKE?

KID WATCHES A LOT OF TV, DOES HE?

BOY, CALVIN TAKES THAT STUFFED TIGER EVERYWHERE HE GOES.

YEAH, THEY'RE INSEPARABLE.

DO YOU WORRY ABOUT THAT? I MEAN, SHOULDN'T HE BE PLAYING WITH REAL FRIENDS?

OH, I THINK HE WILL WHEN HE'S READY. DIDN'T YOU EVER HAVE AN IMAGINARY FRIEND?

SOMETIMES I THINK *ALL* MY FRIENDS HAVE BEEN IMAGINARY.

UNCLE MAX, LOOK! I'LL SHOW YOU A MAGIC DISAPPEARING TRICK!

OK, FIRST I'LL NEED AN ORDINARY TWENTY-DOLLAR BILL.

HOW ABOUT IF I LEND YOU A NICKEL INSTEAD?

NO, IT WORKS MUCH BETTER WITH A TWENTY. ...OR A FIFTY, IF YOU HAVE ONE.

I TAKE IT YOU THINK YOUR OL' UNCLE MAX IS A LOW-WATT BULB.

WHY, DID DAD TELL YOU HOW THIS WORKS?

WHEN ARE YOU GOING BACK HOME, UNCLE MAX?

TOMORROW. IS THAT SOON ENOUGH?

GEE, I WISH YOU COULD STAY FOREVER.

WHAT A NICE THING TO SAY! YOU'RE ALL RIGHT, CALVIN.

MOM'S A LOT MORE PATIENT WITH ME IN FRONT OF GUESTS.

WELL, SO LONG, MAX. IT WAS GREAT TO SEE YOU AGAIN.

YOU, TOO. HAVE A SAFE TRIP HOME.

COME VISIT ME SOMETIME, OK, FELLA?

HECK, I'LL COME RIGHT NOW! SO LONG, MOM! BYE, DAD!

CALVIN, GET BACK HERE!

I NEVER GET TO DO ANYTHING FUN.

MISSED YOUR CHANCE DEAR. WE COULD'VE BOUGHT HIM A TICKET.

WELL...

ARE YOU JUST GOING TO SIT INSIDE ALL DAY?

YOU SHOULD GO PLAY OUTSIDE AND GET SOME FRESH AIR!

AAGHH, I CAN'T BELIEVE WE WERE ASSIGNED TO DO A REPORT TOGETHER.

ALL I CAN SAY IS YOU'D BETTER DO A GREAT JOB! I DON'T WANT TO FLUNK JUST BECAUSE I WAS ASSIGNED A DOOFUS FOR A PARTNER.

A **DOOFUS** ?? WHO TAKES HER SANDWICHES APART AND EATS EACH INGREDIENT SEPARATELY?

WHAT'S WRONG WITH THAT ?!

IT CERTIFIES YOU AS A GRADE "A" NIMROD.

IT DOES **NOT!**

OK, LOOK. WE'VE GOT TO DO THIS DUMB PROJECT TOGETHER, SO WE MIGHT AS WELL GET IT OVER WITH. WHAT ARE WE SUPPOSED TO BE DOING?

WEREN'T YOU EVEN PAYING ATTENTION ?! WHAT WOULD YOU DO IF I WASN'T HERE TO ASK ?? YOU'D FLUNK AND BE SENT BACK TO KINDERGARTEN, THAT'S WHAT!

SAYS YOU! I HEARD THAT SOMETIMES KIDS DON'T PAY ATTENTION BECAUSE THE CLASS GOES AT TOO SLOW OF A PACE FOR THEM. SOME OF US ARE TOO SMART FOR THE CLASS.

OH, RIGHT. YOU'RE **TOO** SMART.

BELIEVE IT, LADY. YOU KNOW HOW EINSTEIN GOT BAD GRADES AS A KID? WELL, **MINE** ARE EVEN **WORSE!**

SO WHAT ARE WE SUPPOSED TO BE DOING?

WE'RE **SUPPOSED** TO BE RESEARCHING THE PLANET MERCURY.

SO WHAT HAVE WE FOUND OUT?

**NOTHING!** I'M NOT GOING TO DO THIS WHOLE THING MYSELF!

YOU'D PROBABLY GOOF IT ALL UP IF YOU DID. LET'S GET STARTED.

YES! **LET'S!**

I'LL BE THE MANAGEMENT, AND YOU CAN BE THE LABOR. FIRST, GET SOME BOOKS.

DOES ANYONE WANT TO TRADE PARTNERS?

**Panel 1:** WE HAVE TO GIVE OUR REPORT ON PLANET MERCURY TODAY. DID YOU DO YOUR HALF?

**Panel 2:** OF COURSE I DID. AND I'LL BET MY HALF MAKES YOUR HALF LOOK PATHETIC.

**Panel 3:** IT HAD **BETTER** BE GOOD... OR ELSE!

**Panel 4:** THE PLANET MERCURY

An Exhaustively Researched Report by Calvin

**Panel 5:** "...AND SO, THE PLANET MERCURY IS A HOT AND BARREN WORLD, THE CLOSEST TO OUR SUN."

**Panel 6:** AND TO TELL US ABOUT THE MYTHOLOGY OF MERCURY, HERE'S MY PARTNER, CALVIN.

**Panel 7:** THANK YOU, THANK YOU! HEY, WHAT A CROWD! YOU LOOK GREAT THIS MORNING...REALLY, I MEAN THAT! GO ON, GIVE YOURSELVES A HAND!

**Panel 8:** YOU KNOW, A FUNNY THING HAPPENED ON THE WAY TO THE LIBRARY YESTERDAY... THIS ISN'T MY FAULT, MISS WORMWOOD!

**Panel 9:** THE PLANET MERCURY WAS NAMED AFTER A ROMAN GOD WITH WINGED FEET.

**Panel 10:** MERCURY WAS THE GOD OF FLOWERS AND BOUQUETS, WHICH IS WHY TODAY HE IS A REGISTERED TRADEMARK OF FTD FLORISTS.

**Panel 11:** WHY THEY NAMED A PLANET AFTER THIS GUY, I CAN'T IMAGINE.

**Panel 12:** ...UM... BACK TO YOU, SUSIE.

BOY, YOU SHOULD'VE SEEN THE SPARKS FLY WHEN I GAVE MY HALF OF THE REPORT.

I'VE NEVER SEEN SUSIE SO MAD. SHE ACCUSED ME OF NOT DOING ANY RESEARCH AND CLAIMED I MADE UP THE WHOLE THING.

DID YOU?

HECK, NO. I JUST TOOK A FEW CREATIVE LIBERTIES.

AND THEY CALLED YOUR MOM OVER A FEW CREATIVE LIBERTIES?

GEEZ, YOU THINK *SUSIE* WAS MAD...

DON'T YOU HATE IT WHEN YOUR BOOGERS FREEZE?

HERE WE ARE, OVERLOOKING SUICIDE GULCH, ABOUT TO HURL OURSELVES DOWN AT BREAKNECK SPEED IN A SLED THAT HARDLY STEERS!

RISKING LIFE AND LIMB! LOOKING DEATH STRAIGHT IN THE EYE!

"WHY?" YOU ASK! WHY DO WE DO IT ??

BECAUSE WE GET PAID, I HOPE.

BECAUSE IT'S THERE!

PLANET BOG — POOLS OF TOXIC CHEMICALS BUBBLE UNDER A CHOKING ATMOSPHERE OF POISONOUS GASES.

...BUT ASIDE FROM THAT, IT'S NOT MUCH LIKE EARTH.

WE FIND SPACEMAN SPIFF STRUGGLING ACROSS THE TERRAIN OF A DISTANT PLANET!

SUDDENLY THE GROUND BEGINS TO SHAKE! A CLOUD OF DUST APPEARS ON THE HORIZON! IT'S A ZORG!!

OUR HERO RUNS FOR COVER, BUT THE ZORG IS INSTANTLY UPON HIM!

SPIFF FIRES HIS BLASTER, BUT THE WEAPON IS USELESS AGAINST THE MONSTER!

THE FEARLESS SPACE EXPLORER IS TAKEN TO THE ZORG'S CAVE, WHERE HE DISCOVERS A VAT OF BOILING WATER! OH NO! OUR HERO IS ABOUT TO BE COOKED ALIVE!

SPIFF'S MIND RACES FURIOUSLY...

WELL? GET IN.

DON'T YOU WANT TO LEAN WAY, WAY OVER, AND TEST HOW HOT THE WATER IS?

# Calvin and Hobbes
## by WATTERSON

I'M GOING OUTSIDE! I'LL BE OUT BACK IF ANYONE WANTS ME! I'LL PROBABLY BE GONE A COUPLE HOURS! I'M LEAVING NOW! I'M GOING! SO LONG! SEE YA LATER! BYE!

STOMP STOMP STOMP STOMP

STOMP STOMP STOMP

HEY SUSIE, LOOK! I FOUND DINOSAUR TRACKS!

PRETTY SCARY, HUH? I'LL BET YOU DIDN'T KNOW THERE WERE DINOSAURS IN THIS NEIGHBORHOOD!

ESPECIALLY NOT DINOSAURS WITH SIZE 5, TREADED TOES.

# CaLViN and HObbEs by WATTERSON

 "MY....DAD...IS... A ...BIG...". HEY!

I THINK WE'D BETTER GET THAT KID TO A PSYCHOLOGIST.

Hey, Calvin, guess what we're doing in gym today. We're wrestling!

Next period you'll be so covered with mat burns you'll need skin grafts! Ha ha ha! See ya then, twinky.

SIGHАННН...

PHYSICAL EDUCATION IS WHAT YOU LEARN FROM HAVING YOUR FACE IN SOMEONE'S ARMPIT RIGHT BEFORE LUNCH.

KAPWIINGGG! IT'S CALVIN, THE HUMAN LIGHT PARTICLE!

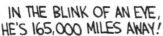

IN THE BLINK OF AN EYE, HE'S 165,000 MILES AWAY!

NOTHING IN THE UNIVERSE IS FASTER THAN CALVIN!

...I HOPE!

MUCH AS I LOVE MY "CHOCOLATE FROSTED CRUNCHY SUGAR BOMBS," THE BEST PART IS AFTER THE CEREAL IS GONE.

THAT'S WHEN YOU EAT THE LEFTOVER MILK THAT'S ALL SLUDGY FROM THE EXTRA SUGAR YOU ADDED.

SOMETIMES I EAT TWO OR THREE BOWLS OF THIS.

I CAN HEAR YOUR HEART RACING FROM HERE.

THEY MAKE THIS CEREAL WITH MARSHMALLOW BITS, TOO, BUT MOM WON'T BUY IT FOR ME.

# Calvin and Hobbes
by WATERSON

IT'S FREEZING UPSTAIRS!

CAN I TAKE SOME LOGS UP TO MY ROOM?

HEY, YOU'RE ON MY SIDE OF THE BED.

THESE SHEETS ARE FREEZING!

YEAH, WELL... AAUGHH! YOUR FEET ARE LIKE ICE! GET AWAY FROM ME!

BUT MY SIDE'S ALL COLD!

WELL DON'T GET ME COLD! MOVE OVER!

SURE, YOU'VE GOT A FUR COAT! I'M JUST WEARING PAJAMAS.

QUIT PULLING THE BLANKETS, WILLYA?

I HARDLY HAVE ANY, YOU HOG! GIMME THOSE!

YOU'RE LETTING IN COLD AIR! QUIT IT! QUIT IT!

SERVES YOU RIGHT, MR. MOSTY-TOASTY! SEE WHAT IT'S LIKE BEING COLD!

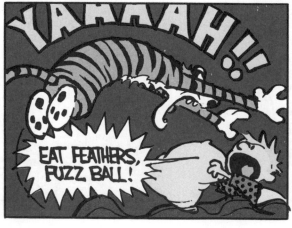

YAAAAH!!

EAT FEATHERS, FUZZ BALL!

WHAP OOF ZPOW

MOVE OVER. YOU'RE GETTING MY SIDE ALL HOT.

OPEN THE WINDOW. I'M ROASTING.

MY SIDE OF THE WOODS ABOUNDS IN NATURAL SCENIC SPLENDOR.

YOUR SIDE WALLOWS IN DECAY AND FILTH. MY TERRITORY IS INFINITELY SUPERIOR TO YOURS.

YOUR SIDE IS SMALLER.

HEY!

I'M HUNGRY.

WELL, YOU CAN'T CATCH ANYTHING IN MY TERRITORY. THAT'S WHAT THE BOOK SAYS.

WHAT DO TIGERS EAT IN THE WILD ANYWAY?

THEY CATCH BIG GROSS CATERPILLARS LIKE THAT ONE.

EWWW. IT'S GOT LITTLE SPIKES ALL OVER HIM. TIGERS REALLY EAT THESE?

BY THE TRUCK LOAD. THEY'RE GREAT.

LET ME SEE THE BOOK.

WHO ARE YOU GOING TO BELIEVE, SOME SILLY WRITER OR A REAL TIGER?

SO FAR, I HAVEN'T HAD MUCH FUN AS A TIGER.

I THOUGHT WE'D BE ROMPING AROUND THE WOODS LIKE WE ALWAYS DO, BUT IT TURNS OUT TIGERS DON'T SHARE THEIR TERRITORIES WITH OTHER TIGERS!

SO HERE WE ARE, SITTING ON OPPOSITE SIDES OF A BIG ROCK. WHAT A BLAST.

BEING A TIGER JUST ISN'T ALL IT'S CRACKED UP TO BE.

THAT'S NOT THE HALF OF IT. IT SAYS HERE WE'RE AN ENDANGERED SPECIES!

# CALVIN AND HOBBES

THE LATE CRETACEOUS PERIOD... WHEN DINOSAURS RULED THE EARTH!

by WATTERSON

..AND CALVIN RULED THE DINOSAURS!

THE TERRIBLE TYRANNOSAURUS SINKS ITS TEETH INTO A TRICERATOPS!

TRIUMPHANT AGAIN, THE UNDISPUTED KING OF DINOSAURS LETS OUT A MIGHTY ROAR!

WITH SAVAGE FEROCITY, THE MONSTER BEGINS ITS FEAST! LIMB-SEVERING, BONE-CRUNCHING AND TENDON-SNAPPING, HE...

CALVIN! THAT'S DISGUSTING!

FOR HEAVEN'S SAKE, SLOW DOWN AND CHEW QUIETLY!

THE TERRIBLE TYRANNOSAURUS RESUMES EATING, MORTIFIED THAT SOMEONE MIGHT SEE HIM.

LIGHTNING FLASHES! THUNDER RUMBLES ACROSS THE SKY!

HORRIBLY, CALVIN HAS BEEN SEWN TOGETHER FROM CORPSES! A POWER SURGE FORCES BLOOD TO HIS BRAIN!

HE'S... HE'S *ALIVE!*

WELL, LOOK WHO'S UP AND ABOUT.

HELLO, SLEEPYHEAD.

..OGGG...

CALVIN WAKES UP STARING INTO THE EYES OF A BIG FROG.

SEEING CALVIN AWAKE, THE FROG SCRAMBLES DOWN AND FORCES OPEN CALVIN'S MOUTH!

CALVIN TRIES TO FIGHT, BUT THE SLIPPERY AMPHIBIAN INSTANTLY SLIDES IN AND IS SWALLOWED! HOW DISGUSTING!

I DON'T FEEL GOOD.

YOU SOUND AWFUL. YOU'VE GOT A FROG IN YOUR THROAT.

CALVIN THE ELEPHANT WANDERS THE AFRICAN PLAIN.

AT FIVE TONS, HE IS THE LARGEST LAND MAMMAL!

HIS DEAFENING CALL SHATTERS THE EARLY-MORNING TRANQUILITY!

A RED SPACESHIP ON THE MONITOR, YOUR VILENESS.

IT'S THAT INFERNAL SPACEMAN SPIFF! OPEN FIRE!

by WATTERSON

SPACEMAN SPIFF IS HIT! HE AIMS FOR PLANET MOK, HOPING TO FIND A REPUTABLE BODY SHOP.

WE JOIN OUR HERO AFTER A CRASH LANDING ON THE HOSTILE PLANET MOK. OMINOUS FIGURES APPEAR ON THE HORIZON!

THE DARING SPACEMAN SPIFF LAYS WASTE WITH HIS DEATH RAY ZORCHER, BUT HE IS HOPELESSLY OUTNUMBERED!

SURROUNDED, OUR HERO IS TAKEN PRISONER, AND CARRIED TO A SUBTERRANEAN DUNGEON!

STILL WON'T TALK, EH, SPIFF? WE'LL SEE ABOUT *THAT!*

YOU'LL NEVER GET ANYTHING FROM ME, SPACE SQUID!

YOU HAD YOUR CHANCE, EARTHLING! TAKE HIM TO THE INTERROGATION ROOM AND *WASH HIS HAIR!*

HA HA HA HA HA

AAUGH! YOU GOT SOAP IN MY EYES ON PURPOSE! SINISTER FIEND!

IF YOU'D STOP THRASHING AROUND, MAYBE IT WOULDN'T HAPPEN!

WATTERSON

# calvin and HOBBES

by WATTERSON

**Calvin:** WILL YOU GET ME A GLASS OF WATER?

**Mom:** YOU JUST HAD ONE.

**Calvin:** I WANT ONE TO KEEP BY THE BED, SO I CAN DOUSE THIS GUY IF HE STARTS SNORING.

**Mom:** GOOD NIGHT, CALVIN.

Z

**Hobbes:** HEE HEE HEE HEE

**Calvin:** OH, GREAT. HE'S DREAMING AGAIN.

SNIFF SNIFF SNIFF

**Hobbes:** WHERE DO YOU THINK YOU ARE, YOU IMBECILE? OUT IN THE JUNGLE?

**Hobbes:** ...MM... HEH HEH HEH

**Calvin:** IF HE STARTS "RUNNING," HE'S GONNA GET A PILLOW IN THE KISSER.

SNIFF SNIFF

**Calvin:** HEY! WHERE ARE YOU GOING??

**Calvin:** SOMNAMBULISTS GIVE ME THE CREEPS. WHY ARE WE GOING TO THE KITCHEN?

Z

**Dad:** CALVIN! WHAT ARE YOU DOING? HAVE YOU BEEN SLEEPWALKING??

**Calvin:** I WAS COMPLETELY AWAKE! IT'S THIS DOPE WHO'S SLEEPWALKING! I JUST FOLLOWED HIM.

**Dad:** I PUT HIM BACK TO BED. HE COULDN'T GIVE ANY REASON FOR BEING UP.

**Mom:** DO YOU SUPPOSE IT MEANS ANYTHING? LOOK, HE GOT OUT ALL THE TUNA!

AHH! LUNCH, MY FAVORITE MEAL! AND TODAY'S LUNCH IS *EXTRA* SPECIAL!

 EVER SINCE THE WEATHER GOT WARM I'VE BEEN SWATTING FLIES AND SAVING THEM IN A JAR.

 FINALLY I GOT ENOUGH BUGS TO MASH THEM INTO A GOOEY PASTE WITH A SPOON.

 I CALL IT "BUG BUTTER." CARE FOR A TASTE? / TELL ME, CALVIN, DO YOU HAVE ANY FRIENDS AT *ALL*?

 OK, YOU'VE ALL READ THE CHAPTER, SO WHO CAN TELL ME WHAT'S IMPORTANT ABOUT THE BATTLE OF LEXINGTON?

 ANYONE?

 CALVIN, HOW ABOUT YOU?

 HARD TO SAY, MA'AM. I THINK MY CEREBELLUM JUST FUSED.

 HEY, MOM, CAN WE GO OUT FOR HAMBURGERS TONIGHT?

 NOT TONIGHT, DEAR. / AW, MOM! WHY NOT?

 BECAUSE I'M ALREADY FIXING SOMETHING FOR DINNER.

 YEAH... I KNOW.

IF YOU WANT TO STAY DAD, YOU'VE GOT TO POLISH YOUR IMAGE.

MY IMAGE.

RIGHT. SEE, NOW EVERYONE THINKS YOU'RE INSENSITIVE TO THE LEGITIMATE NEEDS OF MINORS.

A FEW MAGNANIMOUS GESTURES WHILE IN OFFICE NOW MIGHT BE IN ORDER. IF YOUR MIND'S GONE BLANK, I HAVE SOME SUGGESTIONS.

OH, THE SUSPENSE.

FOR EXAMPLE, YOU MIGHT REPEAL MANDATORY SCHOOL ATTENDANCE. THAT ALONE COULD ROCKET YOU TO VICTORY.

MUCH AS I APPRECIATE YOUR OFFER, I DON'T THINK I NEED AN IMAGE CONSULTANT.

I PREFER TO LET THE WISDOM OF MY WORDS AND DEEDS SPEAK FOR THEMSELVES.

IN THAT CASE, YOU'LL HAVE A LOT OF TIME TO WRITE YOUR MEMOIRS.

WE'LL SEE. NOW IT'S PAST YOUR BEDTIME.

"DAD BURIED IN LANDSLIDE! JUBILANT THRONGS FILL STREETS! STUNNED FATHER INCONSOLABLE— DEMANDS RECOUNT!"

GOOD NIGHT.

EIGHT... NINE... TEN! HERE I COME, READY OR NOT!

ALL RIGHT, GIVE 'EM BACK!

HERE I AM, WAITING FOR THE BUS. ELEVEN MORE YEARS OF SCHOOL TO GO. THEN COLLEGE, THEN MAYBE GRADUATE SCHOOL, AND THEN I WORK UNTIL I DIE.

WHAT KIND OF WORLD *IS* THIS?! YOU ONLY GET FIVE YEARS TO BE A KID??

WHAT ABOUT EXPLORING AND DISCOVERING AND PLAYING? THOSE THINGS ARE IMPORTANT, TOO!

WELL, YOU STILL HAVE AFTERNOONS AND WEEKENDS.

THAT'S WHEN I WATCH TV.

LOOK, HOBBES, I GOT A MODEL AIRPLANE. WANT TO HELP ME BUILD IT?

SURE.

WOW, A PHANTOM JET! I CAN'T WAIT UNTIL IT'S DONE!

LOOK AT ALL THE LITTLE PIECES.

HERE, YOU PUT THOSE PIECES TOGETHER, AND I'LL DO THESE. THEN WE'LL STICK YOURS ON MINE, OK?

SHOULDN'T WE READ THE INSTRUCTIONS?

DO I *LOOK* LIKE A SISSY?

HEY, THESE INSTRUCTIONS ARE IN THREE DIFFERENT LANGUAGES.

UH OH, I GOT GLUE ON MY HANDS.

IT STARTS IN ENGLISH, BUT THEN IT GOES INTO FRENCH AND SPANISH.

THIS STUFF IS WORSE THAN MOZZARELLA CHEESE.

IT'S HARD TO BELIEVE THIS MODEL IS FOR AGES SIX AND UP.

YECCHH. WHAT A MESS.

YOU HAVE TO BE TRI-LINGUAL JUST TO READ THE DIRECTIONS.

I HOPE MOM LIKES THIS NEWSPAPER HERE ON THE FLOOR, BECAUSE IT'S SURE NOT GOING ANY- WHERE.

NUTS! THIS WHEEL STRUT SNAPPED. WHY DO THEY MAKE 'EM SO DARN SMALL?

I GUESS THAT WAS AN OPTIONAL PIECE.

MY WHEEL WON'T FIT IN THE WHEEL WELL.

HERE, LET ME TRY. SOMETIMES YOU JUST HAVE TO...

SNAP

DARN IT!

THIS PLANE IS IN FOR SOME ROUGH LANDINGS.

LOOK AT THIS STUPID MODEL. IT LOOKS AWFUL!

OUR PLANE DOESN'T LOOK ANYTHING LIKE THE PICTURE ON THE BOX.

MAYBE WE CAN FIX IT WHEN WE PAINT IT.

I CAN'T PAINT IT LIKE THIS. LOOK HOW GOOD THEY DID THIS!

HOW'D THEY PAINT EYEBROWS ON A PILOT THAT'S LESS THAN AN INCH TALL??

I THINK THAT'S A REAL JET SUPERIMPOSED ON A PLASTIC STAND.

I HATE THIS MODEL. NOTHING FIT RIGHT, THE INSTRUCTIONS WERE INCOMPREHENSIBLE, THE DECALS RIPPED, THE PAINT SLOPPED, AND THE GLUE GOT EVERYWHERE.

WHAT A DISASTER. SIX BUCKS COMPLETELY DOWN THE DRAIN.

I CAN'T THINK OF AN AFTERNOON I'VE ENJOYED LESS. WHAT A WASTE. WHAT A DUMB HOBBY.

..OF COURSE, WITH THIS FOR PRACTICE, I'LL BET WE COULD DO GREAT ON ANOTHER MODEL!

LET'S GET ONE OF THOSE CLIPPER SHIPS WITH ALL THE RIGGINGS.

# Calvin and Hobbes

by WATTERSON

C'MON, HOBBES. LET ME UP INTO THE TREE FORT.

SAY THE PASSWORD.

NO! YOU KNOW IT'S ME! LET ME UP!

YOU MAY BE SOME OTHER KID IN DISGUISE.

IT'S *ME*, CALVIN! LET ME UP, YOU HAIRBALL BARFER!

AN INSULT! WELL, YOU CAN JUST STAY DOWN THERE *FOREVER*, MR. STINKER.

OH, NO! HERE COMES SUSIE! LET ME UP QUICK, SO WE CAN THROW THINGS AT HER! HURRY! LET DOWN THE ROPE!

LA DE DA DUM DOO ♪ ♫

SHE'S COMING! QUICK! LET DOWN THE ROPE! I'M SORRY I INSULTED YOU! OK? SEE, I SAID I WAS SORRY! CAN'T YOU LET DOWN THE ROPE?!

YOU HAVE TO SAY THE PASSWORD.

..Verse Seven: TIGERS ARE PERFECT, THE *E*-PIT-O-ME OF GOOD LOOKS AND GRACE AND QUIET..UH..UM..DIGNITY..

I WAS GOING TO ASK YOU TO COME OVER AND PLAY HOUSE, BUT I THINK YOU'D BE A WEIRD EXAMPLE FOR OUR CHILDREN.

ONE OF THESE DAYS I'M GOING TO MAKE YOU INTO A RUG! YOU HEAR ME?? A RUG!

CAN I USE THE GARDEN SHOVEL?

WHAT DO YOU WANT IT FOR?

HOBBES AND I ARE GOING ON AN ARCHAEOLOGICAL EXPEDITION.

IF YOU'RE LOOKING FOR FOSSILIZED REMAINS, YOU SHOULD DIG THROUGH YOUR ROOM.

HA HA. SOMEDAY I'LL NAME AN AUSTRALOPITHECUS WOMAN AFTER YOU.

I'VE BEEN READING UP ON PALEONTOLOGY. IT'S AMAZING STUFF.

SCIENTISTS CAN TELL HOW OLD SOMETHING IS JUST BY ANALYZING THE LAYERS OF DIRT IT'S IN.

HEY!

WHY, YOU MUST BE SIX YEARS OLD.

OH, YOU'RE A SCREAM.

ARCHAEOLOGISTS DIG SLOWLY AND CAREFULLY, USING SMALL, DELICATE TOOLS.

EACH ROCK HAS TO BE PAINSTAKINGLY BRUSHED AND SCRAPED SO NOTHING IS BROKEN OR MISSED.

DIG DIG SCRAPE SCRAPE BRUSH BRUSH

ARCHAEOLOGISTS HAVE THE MOST MIND-NUMBING JOB ON THE PLANET.

I DON'T THINK YOUR DAD WILL WANT TO SHAVE WITH THIS TOMORROW.

MOM SAYS SHE DOESN'T THINK WE'VE FOUND A SKELETON AT ALL.

SHE SAYS WE JUST DUG UP SOME TRASH SOMEBODY LITTERED.

OUR DINOSAUR IS A FRAUD.

I GUESS IT WOULDN'T BE RIGHT TO SELL IT TO A MUSEUM THEN.

NOT AT FULL PRICE, ANYWAY.

PSST... SUSIE! CAN I COPY YOUR PAPER?

NO.

CALVIN!

AAAUGHH! I SKINNED MY KNEE! OOH! OW!

AAAUGHHH! OW! OW!

# Calvin and Hobbes
by WATTERSON

THE CALL GOES OUT! WE'RE ON THE MOVE!

UP THROUGH THE WINDING MAZE! FASTER! FASTER!

CALVIN SCRAMBLES UP THE GRAINY TUNNEL!

OUT HE POPS INTO THE BLINDING SUN! CALVIN THE ANT RUSHES DOWN THE HILL TO THE BRICK WALK!

OTHER ANTS RUSH AROUND HIM IN THEIR MAD HURRY! CALVIN TRIES TO KEEP UP!

AT LAST HE REACHES THE MONSTROUS DEAD CATERPILLAR! WITHOUT PAUSING, HE HOISTS IT UP!

THE QUEEN DEMANDS HIS TIRELESS TOIL! CALVIN IS BACK OFF TO THE ANT-HILL AS FAST AS HE CAN GO!

WORK, WORK, WORK! THAT'S ALL I'M GOOD FOR AROUND HERE!

I HARDLY THINK PICKING UP YOUR ROOM ONCE IN A WHILE QUALIFIES YOU AS A SLAVE.

# CALVIN and HOBBES
by WATTERSON

THIS IS CALVIN, YOUR CAPTAIN, SPEAKING...

...JUST TO REASSURE YOU THAT, YES, THERE IS SOMEONE UP FRONT.

CALVIN PILOTS THE JET AIRLINER ACROSS THE COUNTRY AT 35,000 FEET.

HE IS GIVEN CLEARANCE TO LAND. BUT WHAT'S THIS? A PLANE FROM A RIVAL AIRLINE IS MAKING FOR THE SAME RUNWAY TO SHAVE PRECIOUS MINUTES OFF ITS SCHEDULE!

IT'S A 600-MPH GAME OF CHICKEN! CALVIN PULLS BACK ON THE THROTTLE AND LURCHES AHEAD!

THE OTHER PILOT TRIES TO CUT CALVIN OFF WITH A SUDDEN DROP IN ALTITUDE!

CALVIN SWITCHES ON THE "FASTEN SEAT BELT" LIGHT IN THE CABIN, AND DOES A BARREL ROLL!

AT 5 Gs, CALVIN HOPES NOT TO BLACK OUT!

AS THEY CLOSE IN ON THE RUNWAY, THE OTHER PILOT HAS NO CHOICE BUT TO PULL UP AND CIRCLE AROUND AGAIN! CALVIN WINS!

HEY, MOM, IS IT TRUE I COULD GET A PILOT'S LICENSE AT AGE 14?

NO.

LOOK AT DAD, CALMLY EATING HIS DINNER AS IF NOTHING WAS WRONG.

I KNOW HIM. HIS "DAD RADAR" IS BEEPING LIKE CRAZY. HE KNOWS I BROKE *SOMETHING*, HE JUST DOESN'T KNOW *WHAT*. HE CAN'T NAIL ME UNTIL HE KNOWS FOR SURE. HE'LL JUST WAIT. I KNOW HIM.

HE'S GOING TO JUST SIT THERE EATING AND LET ME STEW IN MY OWN GUILT. HE FIGURES SOONER OR LATER I'LL CRACK.

CALVIN?

AAUGH! I DID IT! I DID IT! I'M SORRY! I DIDN'T MEAN TO!!

"PASS THE UH." "THE UH..."

YOU *BROKE* THE BINOCULARS?!

DIDN'T I TELL YOU TO BE EXTRA, EXTRA CAREFUL WITH THEM?? ISN'T THAT EXACTLY WHAT I SAID?! WELL?!

THOSE BINOCULARS WERE BRAND NEW! HAVE YOU NO RESPECT FOR OTHER PEOPLE'S PROPERTY?!?

I HAVE AN IDEA, DAD. LET'S PRETEND I ALREADY FEEL TERRIBLE ABOUT IT, AND THAT YOU DON'T NEED TO RUB IT IN ANY MORE.

I DIDN'T *MEAN* TO BREAK YOUR BINOCULARS, DAD. IT WAS AN ACCIDENT.

(SNIFF) I'M REALLY SORRY. I FELT LIKE I WAS GOING TO BARF ALL AFTERNOON.

WELL, I'M SORRY I YELLED AT YOU LIKE I DID. I SHOULDN'T HAVE BEEN SO ANGRY.

AFTER ALL, IT WAS JUST A PAIR OF BINOCULARS. IN THE BIG SCHEME OF THINGS, THAT'S REALLY NOT SO BAD.

(SNIFF) REALLY?

SURE. ...IN ANOTHER TEN YEARS, YOU'LL PROBABLY BE WRECKING MY *CAR*.

# calvin and hobbes by WATTERSON

zzzzzzzzzzzzz

FILTH! CONTAMINATION! PESTILENCE! HA HA HA!

OF ALL LIVING CREATURES, FEW ARE MORE REPULSIVE THAN CALVIN THE BUG!

HE EXISTS ONLY TO SUCK BLOOD AND TRANSMIT PARASITIC DISEASE!

SEARCHING FOR SOMEONE TO INFECT, CALVIN FLIES LOW OVER THE PICNIC TABLE!

INGREDIENTS: SALT,

HIS SENSITIVE ANTENNAE PICK UP THE SCENT OF HUMAN FLESH!

TOUCHING DOWN, CALVIN INSERTS HIS NEEDLELIKE PROBOSCIS INTO A VEIN! PROTOZOANS IN HIS SALIVA QUICKLY INDUCE PLAGUE!

WILL YOU STOP THAT AWFUL SLURPING?! YOU'RE MAKING ME SICK!

HEY, LOOK! MOM AND DAD ARE THROWING DUFFEL BAGS IN THE CAR. THEY'RE GOING ON VACATION!

AT LAST! FINALLY WE GET THE HOUSE TO OURSELVES! WE CAN STAY UP LATE AND WATCH TV! WE CAN EAT COOKIES FOR DINNER! WE...

WHAT ARE YOU DOING UP HERE STILL? C'MON, LET'S GO.

ME? GO? GO WHERE?

ON VACATION! WHAT HAVE WE BEEN PLANNING ALL MONTH?

WITH YOU AND MOM?? WHAT KIND OF VACATION IS *THAT*?!

SO WHERE ARE WE GOING? I SURE HOPE WE'RE NOT CAMPING AGAIN THIS YEAR.

WELL, WE ARE.

OH, NO! WHY DO WE HAVE TO GO CAMPING?! I *HATE* CAMPING!

SWATTING MOSQUITOES WHILE LYING FROZEN AND CRAMPED ON BUMPY ROCKS, WITH NO TV AND ONLY CANNED FOOD TO EAT, IS *NOT* MY IDEA OF A GOOD TIME!

THAT'S WHY WE BROUGHT BUG SPRAY.

LOOK, JUST LET ME OUT HERE, OK? I'LL HITCH HOME AND SEE YOU WHEN YOU GET BACK, ALL RIGHT?

REMEMBER LAST YEAR, WHEN IT RAINED ALL WEEK? IT POURED SO HARD WE COULDN'T EVEN MAKE A FIRE.

WITHOUT QUESTION, THAT WAS ONE OF THE WORST EXPERIENCES OF MY LIFE.

YES, BUT IT BUILT CHARACTER.

OH SURE.

WHY CAN'T I EVER BUILD CHARACTER AT A MIAMI CONDO OR A CASINO SOMEWHERE?

WELL, HERE WE ARE! HOME AWAY FROM HOME!

OK, CALVIN, YOU GET OUT WITH YOUR MOM, AND I'LL HAND OUR GEAR TO YOU.

NOW DON'T DROP THIS. IT'S VERY...

OOPS.

PLOONK

DON'T WORRY, DAD. IT'S ONLY ABOUT TEN FEET DEEP. I CAN SEE THE CAMERA AND EVERYTHING.

I AM GOING TO FEED YOU TO THE SEA GULLS, KID.

DEAR, YOU CAME HERE TO RELAX.

GOSH, THIS WATER'S COLD! HERE, THAT'S ALL I COULD FIND DOWN THERE. GO GET ME A TOWEL, CALVIN.

IT NEVER FAILS. THE ONE BAG THE KID DUMPS IN THE DRINK HAS ALL THE FRAGILE AND PERISHABLE ITEMS IN IT.

WELL, THE WEEK CAN ONLY IMPROVE FROM HERE.

ONE WOULD LIKE TO THINK SO.

HEY, DAD, DID YOU MEAN TO STACK THE TACKLE BOX AND ALL THIS ON YOUR GLASSES?

BOY, DON'T GO NEAR DAD. WHAT A GROUCH!

I DON'T SEE WHY HE CAN'T BE CIVIL JUST BECAUSE I ACCIDENTALLY DROPPED A DUFFEL BAG OVERBOARD AND HE BROKE HIS GLASSES.

ARE YOU GOING TO TELL HIM HE LEFT THE CAR LIGHTS ON BACK WHERE WE GOT THE CANOE?

I THINK YOU SHOULD TELL HIM.

THIS PROBABLY JUST GOES TO SHOW SOMETHING, BUT I SURE DON'T KNOW WHAT.

THERE'S QUITE A BREEZE UP HERE. I'M REALLY MOVING. THERE'S THE RIVER AND THE TOWN TRIANGLE.

HEY, DOWN THERE! MY NAME IS CALVIN! TELL MY TIGER, HOBBES, I'M BLOWING AWAY ON A BALLOON!

CAN ANYONE HEAR ME? TELL HOBBES HE CAN'T READ MY COMIC BOOKS JUST 'CAUSE I'M NOT AROUND, OK?

..OH, YEAH, TELL MY PARENTS WHAT HAPPENED, TOO, ALL RIGHT? HELLO? HELLO?

UH OH, I'M HEADING INTO A FLOCK OF DUCKS!

EXCUSE ME! COMING THROUGH!

PARDON ME! GANGWAY! BEEP BEEP!

..BOY, IF LOOKS COULD KILL.

MY HANDS ARE GETTING TIRED. I'LL TIE THE BALLOON STRING ONTO MY BELT LOOP.

THERE... WHOOP!

SHOOF

IF A PLANE COMES ALONG NOW, I'M GONNA DIE.

WELL, I SUPPOSE THINGS DON'T GET WORSE THAN HANGING FROM A HELIUM BALLOON A MILE ABOVE SOME UNRECOGNIZED STATE.

OF COURSE, MY GRIP COULD WEAKEN, OR I COULD GET SUCKED INTO A JET INTAKE.

THAT'S ONE OF THE REMARKABLE THINGS ABOUT LIFE. IT'S NEVER SO BAD THAT IT CAN'T GET WORSE.

BOY, I'M JUST GOING HIGHER AND HIGHER.

I SUPPOSE EVENTUALLY THE PRESSURE IN THE BALLOON WILL BE GREATER THAN THE AIR PRESSURE AROUND IT, AND THE BALLOON WILL...

POP!

THIS HAS GOT TO BE A DREAM.

WHENEVER YOU FALL FROM TWO MILES UP IN THE SKY, YOU LOOK DOWN, GASP, AND SUDDENLY WAKE UP.

GASP!

GASP
GASP
GASP
GASP
GASP

I WONDER IF MY LIFE WILL FLASH BEFORE MY EYES.

THAT'S THE PROBLEM WITH BEING SIX YEARS OLD...

...MY LIFE WON'T TAKE VERY LONG TO WATCH.

MAYBE I CAN GET A FEW SLOW-MOTION REPLAYS OF THE TIME I SMACKED SUSIE UPSIDE THE HEAD WITH A SLUSHBALL.

SAY, I WONDER IF I HAVE ANY GUM IN MY POCKET. I COULD BLOW A BIG BUBBLE, AND...

NOPE, NO GUM. LET'S TRY *THIS* POCKET.

MY TRANSMOGRIFIER GUN !!

BOY, THESE THINGS COME IN HANDY ALL THE TIME.

I FORGOT ALL ABOUT MY TRANSMOGRIFIER GUN! NOW I HAVE NOTHING TO WORRY ABOUT!

I'LL JUST POINT IT AT MYSELF AND TRANSMOGRIFY! I'M SAFE!

ZAP

WHERE HAVE YOU BEEN?? I'VE BEEN CALLING AND CALLING. YOUR DINNER'S COLD, I'M SURE.

I DRIFTED AWAY ON MY BALLOON AND IT POPPED, BUT FORTUNATELY I HAD MY TRANSMOGRIFIER, SO AFTER I MISTAKENLY TURNED MYSELF INTO A SAFE, I TRANSMOGRIFIED INTO A LIGHT PARTICLE AND ZIPPED BACK HOME INSTANTANEOUSLY!

...OF COURSE, IF I'D KNOWN WE WERE HAVING *THIS*, I WOULDN'T HAVE HURRIED.

SOMETIME YOU SHOULD TRY TRANSMOGRIFYING YOURSELF INTO SOMEONE WHO OCCASIONALLY MAKES AN OUNCE OF SENSE.

CALVIN, I'D LIKE YOU TO PICK UP ALL THE STICKS AND FALLEN BRANCHES IN THE YARD, SO I CAN MOW IT.

WILL YOU PAY ME?

WELL... OK, I'LL PAY YOU A DOLLAR.

A DOLLAR? I WON'T DO IT FOR LESS THAN TWENTY-FIVE!!

IN A MINUTE YOU'LL DO IT FOR NOTHING, JUST BECAUSE I TOLD YOU TO.

...I'LL TAKE THE DOLLAR.

SMART KID.

WHAT DO YOU THINK OF THE ZOO?

I THINK IT'S KIND OF DEPRESSING.

I ALWAYS FEEL SORRY FOR THE ANIMALS. THEY DON'T HAVE MUCH ROOM TO MOVE, OR ANYTHING TO DO.

THEY JUST SLEEP UNTIL THEY'RE FED.

THAT'S PRETTY MUCH ALL *YOU* DO.

YOU KNOW WHAT I MEAN.

HEY, THOSE KIDS ARE FEEDING THE ANIMALS!

MOM, CAN I GET SOME PEANUTS TO FEED THE ANIMALS?

I'M NOT YOUR MOM.

WHOOP!

ARE YOU LOST? WHAT DOES YOUR MOM LOOK LIKE?

FROM THE KNEES DOWN, SHE LOOKS JUST LIKE YOU.

GOSH, I FOLLOWED THAT LADY HALFWAY AROUND THE ZOO, THINKING SHE WAS MY MOM.

WHY DON'T MOMS WRITE THEIR NAMES ON THEIR CALVES SO THIS KIND OF THING WOULDN'T HAPPEN?

I WONDER WHERE I AM. AND WHERE'S HOBBES? I THOUGHT HE WAS RIGHT WITH ME.

UH OH. WHERE'S CALVIN?

WHY DO THESE LITTLE FAMILY TRIPS ALWAYS TURN OUT THIS WAY? I'M GOING TO SPEND MORE SATURDAYS AT THE OFFICE.

YOU FOUND HIM! THANK GOODNESS! WHERE WAS HE?

LOOKING AT THE TIGERS.

I FOLLOWED ANOTHER LADY, THINKING IT WAS MOM, AND THEN WHEN I REALIZED I WAS LOST, I WENT TO ASK THE TIGERS IF THEY'D SEEN HOBBES.

NEXT TIME YOU SHOULD ASK A *PERSON* FOR HELP.

...OH... THAT NEVER OCCURRED TO ME.

ONLY NEXT TIME, THERE WON'T *BE* A NEXT TIME, BECAUSE WE'RE JUST GOING TO TIE YOU TO A STAKE IN THE YARD EVERY WEEKEND.

DEAR!

A FAT LOT OF HELP YOUR COMPATRIOTS WERE, I MIGHT ADD.

---

DO YOU KNOW WHAT DAY IT IS?

NOPE. WHY?

OH, NO REASON. I WAS JUST CURIOUS.

I SURE LIKE SUMMER VACATION.

---

SO YOU WANT SOME WATER, HUH? WELL, I'VE GOT A BIG CAN OF IT HERE.

IT'S UP TO *ME* TO DECIDE IF YOU GET WATER OR NOT! *I* CONTROL YOUR FATE! YOUR VERY *LIVES* ARE IN MY HANDS!

WITHOUT *ME* YOU'RE AS GOOD AS DEAD! WITHOUT *ME*, YOU DON'T...

# Calvin and Hobbes by WATTERSON

RUSTLE
RUSTLE

ZING!

WHAM!

WE TIGERS JUST *LIVE* FOR THAT!

NOT FOR LONG, YOU WON'T.

# calvin and Hobbes
by WATTERSON

BOY, WHAT A BEAUTIFUL SUMMER MORNING, HUH, DAD? TOO BAD YOU CAN'T STAY HOME TO ENJOY IT.

WHEN YOU'RE OLD, YOU'LL BE SORRY YOU NEVER TOOK ADVANTAGE OF DAYS LIKE THESE, BUT OF COURSE, THAT'S FAR OFF, AND IN THE MEANTIME, THERE'S LOTS OF WORK TO BE DONE.

YEP, YOU'D BETTER GO TO WORK. HAVE A GOOD LONG DRIVE IN TRAFFIC. MAYBE YOU'LL GET HOME IN TIME TO WATCH THE SUN SET... IF YOU CAN STAY AWAKE. SO LONG!

GOLLY, I'D HATE TO HAVE A KID LIKE ME.

WHAT WOULD YOU DO IF I CREAMED YOU WITH THIS WATER BALLOON RIGHT NOW?

TAKE THE WORST THING YOU CAN IMAGINE, AND IMAGINE SOMETHING A HUNDRED TIMES WORSE THAN THAT.

YOU'D DO *THAT*?

NO, I'D DO SOMETHING EVEN WORSE.

HE PIQUED MY CURIOSITY.

BIP

WHEEEE.

203

204

CALVIN and HOBBES by WATTERSON

DINOSAURS EVERYWHERE FLEE FOR THEIR LIVES!

CALVIN IS COMING!

THE LATE CRETACEOUS: THE LAST EPOCH OF THE MIGHTY DINOSAURS!

KING OF THE THUNDER LIZARDS IS THE FEARSOME CALVIN, THE TYRANNOSAURUS!

SEVEN TONS OF MUSCLE AND TEETH, HE SEARCHES FOR PREY!

CALVIN, FOR GOODNESS' SAKE, STOP STOMPING AROUND! YOU'RE DRIVING ME CRAZY!

OW!! CHOMP!

HOW DID THE FEARSOME TYRANNOSAURUS BECOME EXTINCT? NOW WE KNOW!

WATTERSON

208

WAP

IS THIS YOURS?

NO. WHAT IS IT?

FOR A GIRL, SHE'S REMARKABLY PERCEPTIVE.

GIVE ME SOME COOKIES, OR I LIGHT THE FUSE AND SEND US ALL TO KINGDOM COME!

WHAT DID YOU DO, STICK A PIECE OF STRING INTO A HOT DOG? FOR HEAVEN'S SAKE, DON'T WASTE FOOD, CALVIN. GIVE ME THAT.

CAN I HAVE ANY COOKIES?

NO. GO PLAY OUTSIDE.

I SURE WISH I COULD GET MY HANDS ON SOME *REAL* DYNAMITE.

CAN I HAVE THE HOT DOG, OR DID YOUR MOM TAKE IT?

EVERYTHING FLOATS RANDOMLY IN THE ROOM! THERE'S NO GRAVITY!

CALVIN PUSHES OFF THE CEILING AT A SHARP ANGLE, AIMING FOR THE HALLWAY!

HE GLIDES WITH UNCHECKED MOMENTUM, TURNING HIMSELF TO BE ABLE TO PUSH OFF THE NEXT STATIONARY SURFACE.

C'MON, YOU! OUTSIDE! YOU'RE REALLY BOUNCING OFF THE WALLS TODAY.

AW, MOM.

EXTRA PANTS...

THREE SHIRTS, TWO SWEATERS, TWO SWEATSHIRTS...

ANOTHER PAIR OF PANTS...

STILL TRYING TO LEARN TO RIDE THAT BICYCLE, EH?

I DON'T NEED ANY COMMENTS FROM YOU.

A SHADOW FALLS OVER THE LARGE CITY SKYSCRAPERS!

IT'S A GIGANTIC ANT! WITH ONE FOOTSTEP, IT PULVERIZES THE ENTIRE DOWNTOWN! MILLIONS DIE INSTANTLY!

THE ANT BRUSHES THE CITY OFF THE MAP! PEOPLE FLOOD THE STREETS IN PANIC, ONLY TO BE SMASHED IN THE HORRIBLE WRECKAGE!

WELL... MAYBE I WON'T...

TRIP

BAP

WHACK

BAP

I'M HUNGRY.

TOO BAD. BREAKFAST ISN'T UNTIL TOMORROW.

MY TUMMY'S GROWLING.

HUSH.

MOST PEOPLE DON'T SLEEP WELL NEXT TO A HUNGRY TIGER.

SOMETIMES I SURE WISH I HAD A DOG.

MORE TUNA AND LESS MAYONNAISE.

OH, NO! THERE'S A TYRANNOSAURUS IN THE GROCERY STORE!

THE DINOSAUR HEADS FOR THE MEAT DEPARTMENT AND DEVOURS THE BUTCHER!

SHOPPERS EVERYWHERE FLEE FOR THEIR LIVES! IT'S MAYHEM, DESTRUCTION AND CARNAGE IN THE AISLES!

OH, NO! CALVIN, CAN'T I TAKE YOU ANYWHERE?!

NOW THE TYRANNOSAURUS WANTS COOKIES!

**Row 1:**

PLANET CALVIN MOVES ACROSS THE SOLAR SYSTEM.

NOBODY NOTICES UNTIL HIS ORBIT TAKES HIM DIRECTLY BETWEEN THE SUN AND EARTH.

CALVIN CAUSES A TOTAL SOLAR ECLIPSE! EARTH IS SHROUDED IN DARKNESS. HOW LONG WILL CALVIN STAY THERE?!

COULD YOU MOVE, PLEASE? YOU'RE IN MY LIGHT.

HA HA HAAA!

**Row 2:**

ELECTION DAY IS COMING UP. HAVE YOU DECIDED ON A RUNNING MATE?

A RUNNING MATE?

SURE. YOU CAN'T BE ELECTED DAD WITHOUT A MOM, RIGHT?

ARE YOU GOING TO KEEP THE MOM I'VE HAD, OR GET A *NEW* RUNNING MATE?

GEE...

BEDTIME, CALVIN.

OF COURSE I'LL STICK WITH YOUR MOM.

AWW...

**Row 3:**

I THINK RITUALS ARE IMPORTANT.

*MY* FAVORITE RITUAL IS EATING THREE BOWLS OF "CHOCOLATE FROSTED SUGAR BOMBS" AND WATCHING TV CARTOONS ALL SATURDAY MORNING.

AFTER A FEW HOURS, I'M SO OVERSTIMULATED I CAN'T SIT STILL OR EVEN THINK STRAIGHT.

SORT OF A TRANSCENDENTAL EXPERIENCE, HUH?

YEAH. I ACHIEVE A LOWER CONSCIOUSNESS.

ALL RIGHT, ALL RIGHT! I'M *GOING!*

HEY! LEGGO! I CAN WALK MYSELF! I JUST HAVE TO... *OK!* LOOK, I'M GOING! I'M GOING!

SURE, YOU THINK SCHOOL'S GREAT *NOW*, BUT IN A COUPLE OF HOURS YOU'LL *MISS* ME! YOU'LL SEE!

THERE GOES CALVIN OFF TO SCHOOL. HE SURE PUT UP A FUSS.

WELL, HE'LL HAVE FUN ONCE HE GETS THERE.

SEE, HE'S EVEN RUNNING NOW. HE'S ALL EXCITED ABOUT...

HEY! CALVIN, THE BUS STOP IS *THAT* WAY! COME BACK HERE!

I CAN'T BELIEVE I'M HERE WAITING TO GO TO SCHOOL. WHAT HAPPENED TO SUMMER?

GOSH, I COULDN'T *WAIT* FOR TODAY! SOON WE'LL BE MAKING NEW FRIENDS, LEARNING ALL SORTS OF IMPORTANT THINGS, AND...

WHAT'S THE MATTER WITH *YOU??*

YOUR BANGS DO A GOOD JOB OF COVERING UP THE LOBOTOMY STITCHES.

I PLEDGE ALLEGIANCE...

TO QUEEN FRAGG... AND HER MIGHTY STATE OF HYSTERIA...

IT'S GOING TO BE A LONG YEAR.

NCIPAL

Hey, Calvin, you're on my swing. Get lost.

I'M NOT SCARED OF YOU, MOE.

Oh no?

NOPE. YOU'RE SO DUMB YOU PROBABLY NEVER THOUGHT ABOUT HOW A SPARROW'S SMALLER SIZE AND GREATER MANEUVERABILITY IS AN ADVANTAGE IN FIGHTING OFF BIG CROWS.

Yeah?

PUNCH

THOSE TV NATURE PROGRAMS WILL BE THE DEATH OF ME YET.

YES, CALVIN?

MAY I BE EXCUSED, PLEASE?

AGAIN?

I HAVE TO GO. BAD.

ALL RIGHT.

THANK YOU.

WHAT ARE YOU DOING HOME?!

I HAD TO GO.

# Calvin and Hobbes

by WATTERSON

SCHOOL'S OUT! FREE AT LAST!

AND JUST SIX PRECIOUS HOURS BEFORE BED TO FORGET EVERYTHING I LEARNED TODAY.

I HATE COMING HOME FROM SCHOOL. I NEVER KNOW IF HOBBES IS WAITING TO POUNCE ON ME.

MAYBE I CAN STAND OFF TO THE SIDE HERE, AND PUSH THE DOOR OPEN WITH A STICK.

I'M HOME!

WHAT DO YOU DO, WAIT UNTIL YOU SEE THE WHITES OF MY EYES?!?

BOY, YOU SHOULD'VE **SEEN** THEM! THEY WERE AS BIG AS DINNER PLATES! HOO HOO HOO!

HAVE YOU BEEN READING THE PAPERS? GROWN-UPS REALLY HAVE THE WORLD FOULED UP.

ACID RAIN, TOXIC WASTES, HOLES IN THE OZONE, SEWAGE IN THE OCEANS, AND ON AND ON!

THE ONLY BRIGHT SIDE TO ALL THIS IS THAT EVENTUALLY THERE MAY NOT BE A PIECE OF THE PLANET WORTH FIGHTING OVER.

YOU'RE PACKING?

YEP. GET YOUR TOOTHBRUSH, HOBBES. WE'RE OUTTA HERE.

IT'S AN OUTRAGE HOW GROWN-UPS HAVE POLLUTED THE EARTH! I REFUSE TO INHERIT A SPOILED PLANET! I'M LEAVING!

REALLY? WHERE TO??

YOU KNOW, SOMETIMES YOU'RE A REAL LOAD TO HAVE AROUND.

I WAS JUST ASKING!

HOW ABOUT MARS? WE COULD GO THERE TO AVOID EARTH'S POLLUTION.

YEAH! IF WE GO NOW, WE CAN CLAIM IT AND KEEP EVERYONE ELSE OFF IT.

OK, IT'S SETTLED. MARS IT IS.

YOU FINISH PACKING. I'LL GO GET THE WAGON.

WE'RE GOING IN THE WAGON?

OF COURSE! WHAT DID YOU WANT TO DO? FLAP YOUR ARMS?

I GUESS I HADN'T THOUGHT ABOUT THAT PART.

OBVIOUSLY.

SPACE TRAVEL MAKES YOU REALIZE JUST HOW SMALL WE REALLY ARE.

WHEN YOU SEE EARTH AS A TINY BLUE SPECK IN THE INFINITE REACHES OF SPACE, YOU HAVE TO WONDER ABOUT THE MYSTERIES OF CREATION.

SURELY WE'RE ALL PART OF SOME GREAT DESIGN, NO MORE OR LESS IMPORTANT THAN ANYTHING ELSE IN THE UNIVERSE. SURELY EVERYTHING FITS TOGETHER AND HAS A PURPOSE, A REASON FOR BEING. DOESN'T IT MAKE YOU WONDER?

*I* WONDER WHAT HAPPENS IF YOU THROW UP IN ZERO GRAVITY.

MAYBE YOU SHOULD WONDER WHAT IT'S LIKE TO WALK HOME.

HANG ON! WE'RE COMING IN THROUGH MARS' ATMOSPHERE.

BONK
BONK

WE'VE LANDED! WE'RE THE FIRST ONES TO EVER SET FOOT ON ANOTHER PLANET! WHAT A HISTORIC MOMENT!

I STILL CAN'T BELIEVE YOU FORGOT THE CAMERA.

*I* REMEMBERED IT. *YOU* JUST DIDN'T WANT TO TURN AROUND.

SEE ANY SIGNS OF MARTIAN LIFE?

NOT YET...

HEY, LOOK! IT'S THE OLD "VIKING" SPACECRAFT THAT LANDED HERE IN THE '70s!

GOSH, I WONDER IF IT'S STILL WORKING.

BLAHHHH HOOP HOOP
BOOLA ACKACKACK
BOOLA

*THAT* OUGHT TO BLOW SOME CIRCUITS AT NASA!

HEE HEE HEE! I'VE ALWAYS WANTED TO DO SOMETHING LIKE THAT.

WELL, THIS IS OUR NEW HOME. I GUESS WE SHOULD UNPACK AND SET UP CAMP.

COMIC BOOKS... COMIC BOOKS... TUNA... SOME CANDY BARS... MORE TUNA... TOOTHBRUSHES... A CAN OPENER... LOOKS LIKE WE'RE ALL SET.

WHAT'S THIS?

A NIGHT LIGHT. I THOUGHT IT MIGHT BE SCARY SLEEPING ON A NEW PLANET.

BOY, YOU THOUGHT OF EVERYTHING.

NOW WE HAVE TO FIND AN OUTLET.

YEP, MARS MAY BE A LITTLE DULL, BUT IT'S BETTER THAN EARTH.

CRUNCH CRUNCH

WE'VE GOT A WHOLE PLANET TO OURSELVES. BRAND NEW AND UNSPOILED. NO PEOPLE, NO POLLUTION.

NOTHING BUT RUGGED, NATURAL BEAUTY AS FAR AS THE EYE CAN SEE.

THAT'S NOT YOUR CANDY BAR WRAPPER OVER THERE, IS IT?

IT WAS JUST THERE A MINUTE! I WASN'T GOING TO LEAVE IT.

I DON'T KNOW ABOUT YOU, BUT I LIKE IT HERE ON MARS.

I DO TOO. IT'S VERY PEACEFUL.

NOT ONLY THAT, BUT WE DON'T HAVE MOM HERE TO BOSS US AROUND! NO EARLY BEDTIME, NO BATHS, NO DISGUSTING DINNERS, NO...

DID THAT ROCK JUST MOVE??

MOMMMMM!!

I GUESS WE SHOULD GO HOME TO EARTH.

YEAH, WE MAY NOT BE WELCOME HERE.

WE OUGHT TO FIX UP OUR OWN PLANET BEFORE WE GO MESSING AROUND WITH OTHER PEOPLE'S PLANETS.

AFTER ALL, THERE'S ONLY ONE EARTH, AND IT'S GOT TO LAST US A WHILE.

WE ALSO SHOULD GO HOME BECAUSE WE'RE CLEAN OUT OF TUNA.

I HOPE MOM AND DAD DIDN'T RENT OUT MY ROOM.

THERE'S EARTH! WE'RE ALMOST HOME!

LOOK, YOU CAN SEE THE CONTINENTS.

HMM... IF I REMEMBER MY ATLAS, WE LIVE IN A BIG, PURPLE COUNTRY.

AND OUR HOUSE IS BY THE GIANT LETTER "E" IN THE WORD "STATES".

HI, DAD! GUESS WHAT HOBBES AND I DID! WE WENT TO MARS!

WELL, WELL.

YEP. WE WERE GOING TO LIVE THERE BECAUSE EARTH IS SO POLLUTED, BUT WE DISCOVERED THAT MARS IS INHABITED, SO WE CAME BACK HOME.

YOU DIDN'T LIKE THE MARTIANS?

NO, THEY DIDN'T LIKE US. I THINK THEY WERE AFRAID WE'D JUNK UP MARS THE WAY WE'VE JUNKED UP EARTH.

WHAT'S MY GOOD BRIEFCASE DOING OUT, AND WHY DOES IT SMELL LIKE TUNA FISH?!

AND CAN YOU BELIEVE IT, DAD? WE GO CLEAR TO MARS, AND DUMB OL' HOBBES FORGETS THE CAMERA!

**Row 1, Panel 1:** HI SUSIE! GUESS WHAT I BROUGHT FOR LUNCH.

**Row 1, Panel 2:** NO! GO SIT BY SOMEONE ELSE, OK? YOU ALWAYS SAY YOUR LUNCH IS SOMETHING REVOLTING, AND I DON'T WANT TO HEAR IT!

**Row 1, Panel 3:** GEE WHIZ, WHAT'S WRONG WITH YOU? MY LUNCH IS PEANUT BUTTER. WHAT'S SO DISGUSTING ABOUT THAT?!

**Row 1, Panel 4:** HMPH. I'M GLAD THAT ONE DAY OUT OF THE YEAR YOU CAN BE CIVIL.

IT'S MY *DESSERT* THAT'S GROSS! LOOK, A THERMOS FULL OF PHLEGM!

**Row 2, Panel 1:** CALVIN, WILL YOU RUN AND GET MY PURSE, PLEASE? I NEED THE CALCULATOR.

SURE.

**Row 2, Panel 2:** HERE YOU ARE.

THANKS.

**Row 2, Panel 3:** AHEM.

**Row 2, Panel 4:** I'M NOT GOING TO TIP YOU!!

HUH! SEE IF I EVER FETCH ANYTHING AGAIN.

**Row 3, Panel 1:** ELECTION DAY IS COMING UP, DAD. PEOPLE WANT TO KNOW WHERE YOU STAND ON THE ISSUES.

**Row 3, Panel 2:** SUCH AS?

LATER BEDTIMES, EXPANDED TV PRIVILEGES, SHORTER SCHOOL WEEKS, AND LESS DISCIPLINE.

**Row 3, Panel 3:** I'M AGAINST THEM ALL.

I SEE.

**Row 3, Panel 4:** HOW'S YOUR IRA? PRETTY WELL FUNDED?

GO TO BED.

# CALVIN and HOBBES

by WATTERSON

UH-OH.

---

SOMETHING IS VERY WRONG HERE.

---

CALVIN HAS MYSTERIOUSLY SHRUNK TO A QUARTER OF AN INCH TALL!

---

HOW CAN HE MAKE HIS PLIGHT KNOWN TO HIS PARENTS WHEN HE'S SMALLER THAN A PENNY?

---

CALVIN GETS AN IDEA! HE GRABS THE LEG OF OF A PASSING HOUSEFLY AND FLIES TO HIS DAD'S CAMERA!

---

ONCE THERE, HE CLIMBS UP AND SETS THE SELF-TIMER.

---

JUMPING ON THE SHUTTER, CALVIN HAS FIFTEEN SHORT SECONDS TO GET IN FRONT OF THE LENS!

---

WITH LUCK, CALVIN'S DAD WILL HAVE THE FILM DEVELOPED SOON, AND DISCOVER WHAT HAS HAPPENED!

---

WHAT HAPPENED?! LOOK AT ALL THESE TERRIBLE PICTURES! I DON'T REMEMBER TAKING THESE. WHO'S THAT LITTLE SPECK IN THE DISTANCE ALL THE TIME? YOU HAVEN'T BEEN FOOLING WITH MY CAMERA, HAVE YOU?

ME? HECK, NO. MAYBE YOU SHOULD GET THE CAMERA FIXED.

I THINK THE WORST OF THIS IS OVER, SO JUST TRY TO GET SOME SLEEP.

I'M GOING BACK TO BED, BUT GIVE ME A CALL IF YOU FEEL SICK AGAIN, OK? NOW GET SOME REST.

MM HMM.

POOR LITTLE KID.

YECCHHH! THERE IS NOTHING WORSE THAN A SICK ROOMMATE! FACE *THAT* WAY!

IT'S SCARY BEING SICK... ESPECIALLY AT NIGHT.

WHAT IF SOMETHING IS *REALLY* WRONG WITH ME, AND I HAVE TO GO TO THE HOSPITAL??

WHAT IF THEY STICK ME FULL OF TUBES AND HOSES? WHAT IF THEY HAVE TO OPERATE? WHAT IF THE OPERATION FAILS? WHAT IF THIS IS MY... MY... LAST NIGHT...*ALIVE??*

THEN I CAN LOOK FORWARD TO HAVING THE BED TO MYSELF TOMORROW.

FEW THINGS ARE LESS COMFORTING THAN A TIGER WHO'S UP TOO LATE.

FEELING ANY BETTER THIS MORNING, CALVIN?

NO.

I GUESS I'D BETTER MAKE YOU AN APPOINTMENT WITH THE DOCTOR.

OK.

IT'S SATURDAY, BY THE WAY. YOU WON'T MISS SCHOOL.

I KNOW.

WELL, IT LOOKS LIKE CALVIN JUST CAUGHT THE BUG GOING AROUND. NOTHING SERIOUS.

KEEP AN EYE ON HIM, AND LET ME KNOW IF HE ISN'T FEELING BETTER SOON.

OK. THANK YOU.

SO LONG, CALVIN. YOU WERE A GOOD PATIENT THIS TIME.

MM.

NOTHING LIKE A LITTLE VIRUS TO TAKE THE EDGE OFF A KID.

I'D STILL RATHER LET HIS TEACHER DEAL WITH HIM.

I GET TO STAY HOME FROM SCHOOL TODAY.

I GET TO LIE IN BED, DRINK TEA, AND READ COMIC BOOKS ALL DAY.

I WISH I COULD DO THIS EVERY DAY.

...LIKE SOME PEOPLE I KNOW.

YOUR MOM DOESN'T BRING ME TEA IN BED.

I WANT SOME MORE TOAST.

ROOM SERVICE!!

HA! THAT SURE GOT YOU UP HERE QUICK!

TOMORROW YOU'RE GOING TO SCHOOL.

I THINK PEOPLE WORRY TOO MUCH ABOUT LITTLE THINGS.

ALL THEY DO IS MAKE THEMSELVES UNHAPPY THAT WAY.

WHY GET AN ULCER OVER THINGS THAT DON'T REALLY MATTER?

LIKE THE BOOK REPORT YOU'RE SUPPOSED TO BE WRITING NOW ON THE BOOK YOU HAVEN'T READ?

EXACTLY. CASE IN POINT.

WHY IN THE WORLD AM I WAITING IN THE POURING RAIN FOR THE SCHOOL BUS TO TAKE ME SOMEWHERE I DON'T EVEN WANT TO GO?

I GO TO SCHOOL, BUT I NEVER LEARN WHAT I WANT TO KNOW.

I HATE SCHOOL.

EACH DAY I COUNT THE HOURS UNTIL SCHOOL'S OVER. THEN I COUNT THE DAYS UNTIL THE WEEKEND. THEN I COUNT THE WEEKS UNTIL THE MONTH IS OVER, AND THEN THE MONTHS UNTIL SUMMER.

I ALWAYS HAVE TO POSTPONE WHAT I *WANT* TO DO FOR WHAT I *HAVE* TO DO!

WELCOME TO THE WORLD.

WOULD YOU SIGN THIS PARENTAL EXCUSE TO GET ME OUT OF THE NEXT 11½ YEARS OF SCHOOL?

# calvin and Hobbes
by WATTERSON

THE VALIANT SPACEMAN SPIFF, INTERGALACTIC EXPLORER, COMES IN OVER THE MOUNTAINS OF A STRANGE PLANET!

OUR HERO DESPERATELY HOPES TO FIND A REST AREA WITH WORKING FACILITIES.

SPACEMAN SPIFF LANDS ON THE DISTANT PLANET ZOKK!

CLIMBING DOWN FROM HIS SPACECRAFT, OUR HERO PREPARES TO EXPLORE THE SURFACE!

UNEXPECTEDLY, SPIFF'S FIRST STEP SENDS HIM CAREENING THROUGH THE SKY!

SPIFF QUICKLY REALIZES THAT PLANET ZOKK HAS ONLY A FRACTION OF EARTH'S GRAVITY!

OOF

WITH PRACTICE, OUR HERO SOON FINDS HE CAN BOUND EFFORTLESSLY ACROSS THE LANDSCAPE!

STOP BOUNCING ON THE BED AND GO TO SLEEP!

DUMB BALLOON.

POOF POOF

POOF POOOF

POOFF

HEY, SUSIE, DID YOU HAVE ANY TROUBLE WITH OUR MATH HOMEWORK LAST NIGHT?

NO, WHY?

I THOUGHT A COUPLE OF THESE WERE TRICKY. CAN I CHECK MY ANSWERS WITH YOURS?

OK.

THANKS. WHAT DID YOU GET FOR QUESTION ONE?

SEVEN.

SEVEN? GOOD, THAT'S WHAT I GOT. WHAT DID YOU GET FOR QUESTION TWO?

DROP DEAD, CALVIN.

EVER SIT AND WATCH ANTS?

LOOK AT THIS ONE. HE'S CARRYING A CRUMB THAT'S BIGGER THAN HE IS, AND HE'S *RUNNING*.

AND IF YOU PUT AN OBSTACLE IN FRONT OF HIM, HE'LL SCRAMBLE LIKE CRAZY UNTIL HE GETS ACROSS IT. HE DOESN'T LET ANYTHING STOP HIM.

I JUST CAN'T IDENTIFY WITH THAT KIND OF WORK ETHIC.

# CaLViN and HobbEs

by WATTERSON

I FEEL A BIG SNEEZE WELLING UP.

...WHICH IS ALWAYS A SURE SIGN THAT I'M NOT CARRYING A HANDKERCHIEF.

AH...AH...AH..

CHOOOOO!!

MOM, I SNEEZED AND BLEW MY HEAD OFF!

PULL YOUR SHIRT DOWN, CALVIN. YOU'RE NOT FOOLING ANYONE.

MOM WOULD BE A LOT MORE FUN IF SHE WAS A LITTLE MORE GULLIBLE.

JUST THINK, EARTH WAS A CLOUD OF DUST 4.5 BILLION YEARS AGO...

3 BILLION YEARS AGO, THE FIRST BACTERIA APPEARED. THEN CAME SEA LIFE, DINOSAURS, BIRDS, MAMMALS, AND, FINALLY, A MILLION YEARS AGO, MAN.

NOW IN 1988, THERE'S ME.

...THE ACME OF EVOLUTION.

OH, *PLEASE*.

IT'S NOT QUITE THE SAME, IS IT?

AND IT PROBABLY WON'T SNOW FOR ANOTHER MONTH AT LEAST.

Z Z

GRRRR Z

GROWLL RRR!

PSST! HEY! WAKE UP! YOU'RE DREAMING!

GRRRR..

AND MOM WONDERS WHY I NEVER LOOK RESTED IN THE MORNING.

CALVIN, TAKE OFF YOUR OUTFIT BEFORE YOU SIT AT THE TABLE, OK?

CALVIN? WHO'S CALVIN? I'M *STUPENDOUS MAN!*

STOP BEING SILLY, AND DO AS I ASKED YOU.

BUT MOM, I *NEED* TO WEAR THIS FOR DINNER!

NO YOU DON'T. LET'S GO.

BUT STUPENDOUS MAN HAS A STOMACH OF STEEL!

MOM SAID I CAN'T GO OUTSIDE UNTIL I FINISH MY HOMEWORK. IF YOU'LL HELP ME, I'LL BE DONE FASTER. WHAT'S FIVE PLUS SEVEN?

I DON'T KNOW.

I DON'T EITHER.

THEN WRITE, "I DON'T KNOW."

HEY, THAT'S A TRUE ANSWER, ISN'T IT! I CAN WRITE THAT FOR *ALL* OF THESE! WE'RE DONE!

WE'D BETTER HAVE A LOOK AT OUR PRODIGY'S HOMEWORK.

WANT TO GO PLAY OUTSIDE?

NO. I'M WATCHING TV.

YOU HATE THIS SHOW. LET'S GO OUT.

NAH.

WHY NOT?

DAD FINALLY SAID HE WAS SICK OF ARGUING WITH ME, AND FOR ALL HE CARED, I COULD WATCH TV UNTIL MY BRAINS OOZED OUT MY EARS.

SO YOU'RE GOING TO?

IT WAS A HARD-WON PRIVILEGE.

# Calvin and Hobbes

by WATERSON

RINGGG

WHAT A DAY.

YOU THINK THAT'S FUNNY? COME BACK AND FIGHT, YOU WEASEL!

WHAT HAPPENED TO *YOU*???

DON'T ASK. I'M GOING UPSTAIRS TO CHANGE.

CALVIN'S ROOM · ENTER & DIE

NOT AGAAINN.

WHERE'S CALVIN?

I SENT HIM TO HIS ROOM. I CAUGHT HIM MAKING PRANK CALLS TO PET STORES, ASKING IF THEY'D BUY HIS TIGER.

HEY, SUSIE, CAN I BORROW YOUR BLACK CRAYON?

OK, BUT DON'T BREAK IT, AND DON'T PEEL THE PAPER OFF, AND COLOR WITH ALL SIDES OF IT SO IT STAYS POINTY.

GEEZ, WHY DON'T YOU TAKE OUT AN INSURANCE POLICY ON IT?

JUST DON'T RUIN MY CRAYON. WHAT ARE YOU DRAWING ANYWAY?

BLACK BEARS ATTACKING A BLACK FOREST CAMPGROUND AT MIDNIGHT.

GIVE ME MY CRAYON BACK.

HEY! WHAT'S THIS STUFF IN MY SOUP?! YECCHH! IS THIS RICE?!? IT HAD BETTER *NOT* BE!

RICE? LET ME SEE.

LOOK! THESE LITTLE WHITE THINGS! SEE, THERE'S RICE IN MY SOUP! I HATE RICE!

I DIDN'T PUT ANY RICE IN. THOSE ARE MAGGOTS.

EWW WW!

ANOTHER LOVELY MEAL AT HOME WITH MY FAMILY. ...I WISH MY JOB REQUIRED MORE TRAVEL.

WELL, HE'S *EATING* IT NOW, RIGHT?

GOSH, WAIT 'TIL I TELL EVERYONE AT SCHOOL WHAT *WE* HAD FOR DINNER!

UH OH.

HOOP

EEP!

I'VE GOT THE HICCUPS SOMETHING TERRIBLE, MOM.

DRINK SOME WATER.

WHEN I GROW UP, I WANT TO BE AN INVENTOR. FIRST I WILL INVENT A TIME MACHINE.

THEN I'LL COME BACK TO YESTERDAY

AND TAKE MYSELF TO TOMORROW

AND SKIP THIS DUMB ASSIGNMENT.

MOMMM, I'M HOME FROM SCHOOL! OPEN THE DOOR FOR ME, OK?

WHAT'S THE MATTER? IT WASN'T LOCKED.

SOMETIMES HOBBES IS WAITING TO POUNCE ON ME AS SOON AS I OPEN THE DOOR.

OH FOR HEAVEN'S SAKE! FROM NOW ON, DON'T CALL ME TO COME TO THE DOOR UNLESS IT'S LOCKED.

HA! I SURE OUT-SMARTED HOBBES *THIS* TIME!

THBBPTT!

SISSY.

BOY, I'M IN A BAD MOOD TODAY! EVERYONE HAD BETTER STEER CLEAR OF ME!

I HATE *EVERYBODY!* AS FAR AS I'M CONCERNED, EVERYONE ON THE PLANET CAN JUST DROP DEAD. PEOPLE ARE SCUM.

WELL-L-L? DOESN'T ANYONE WANT TO CHEER ME UP?!?

I WISH IT WOULD SNOW EIGHT FEET IN THE NEXT FIVE MINUTES SO THEY'D HAVE TO CLOSE SCHOOL.

C'MON, SNOW! SNOW SNOW SNOW SNOW SNOW SNOW SNOW SNOW!

SO CLOSE... AND YET SO FAR.

DO YOU THINK GOD LETS YOU PLEA BARGAIN?

I'D WORRY MORE ABOUT YOUR MOM.

HELLO?

HI, DAD! IT'S ME, CALVIN. WILL YOU TELL ME A STORY?

CALVIN, I'M AT WORK! I DON'T HAVE TIME TO TELL YOU A STORY NOW! I'M VERY BUSY! GET OFF THE PHONE. I'M EXPECTING IMPORTANT CALLS.

OK, DAD. I'LL JUST STAY HERE QUIETLY GROWING UP AT AN UNBELIEVABLE RATE, NEVER SPENDING MUCH SPECIAL TIME WITH MY OWN DAD, WHO'S ALWAYS WORKING.

RIGHT, RIGHT. THIS IS THE STORY OF THE HYDRAULIC PUMP (Fig. 1), THE WHEEL SHAFT FLANGE (Fig. 2), AND THE EVIL PATENT INFRINGEMENT.

I WANT A GOOD STORY.

# The End